How To Use

MAIL DROPS

For Profit, Privacy And Self-Protection

Second Edition — Revised and Expanded

Jack Luger

Breakout Productions
Port Townsend, Washington

How To Use Mail Drops For Profit, Privacy, And Self-Protection: Second Edition — Revised and Expanded

© 1999 by Breakout Productions

Published by:
Breakout Productions, Inc.
PO Box 1643
Port Townsend, WA 98368

ISBN 1-893626-12-1
Library of Congress Card Catalog 99-60232

Contents

Introduction to Part II

Introduction to Part III

Introduction

Mail drops, also known as "letter boxes," "accommodation addresses," "remail services," and "mail-forwarding services," play important roles in American life. Many people encounter them without realizing what they are. Basically, they're small businesses which allow their clients to use their addresses for a fee. They receive mail for them, and some forward mail to their clients for an additional charge. There are also other services available, depending on the operator. Clients in turn, have various reasons for using addresses which are not their own. All have to do with secrecy. Some are absolutely legal and aboveboard. Others are questionable. Some are downright criminal, because their owners take part in postal scams.

Commercial mail drops began when the post office became unable to keep up with the demand for postal boxes. In some cases, there was a two-year waiting list of people who wanted to rent post office boxes. At first, private mail boxes rented for more than post office boxes because people were willing to pay the premium not to have to wait for a postal box to become available. Today, with over 1,500 mail drops operating in the United States, prices have become more competitive, and in some areas match post office rates.

Service is very competitive with the post office, as private mail drops offer other package services and sell supplies. Many offer longer business hours than the post office.

A study of mail drops (known as "Commercial Mail Receiving Agencies" by the U.S. Postal Service) and their clients is a fascinating eye-opener, even for the person who never contemplates either using one or starting his own. Mail drops attract a variety of clients, some with ordinary and even drab motives, while others fit the label "exotic" very well. Finally, we'll study how some people use mail drops to protect themselves against various postal scams.

The day-to-day operation of a mail drop is very routine. Paper processing is not likely to make anyone's pulse race or blood boil. However, it's often profitable to both operator and client.

Mail drops have also become a political issue. The United States Postal Service sees them as a source of potential abuse and even criminality, and has a number of regulations and practices which some people feel are attacks on privacy and personal liberty. There have been at least two recent court cases over this issue.[1]

This book provides an outline of the services available from mail drops. Part I discusses mail drops generally, and sketches in their place in the scheme of things.

Part II discusses "Mail drops and you." It will tell you how to find one, how to negotiate the services needed, and how to check the mail drop out for reliability. In Part II you'll find specific applications for mail drops, and information on how to use them for various purposes. This part also presents a number of other choices open to you when you seek mail privacy. Some of these choices are more costly, and some cost you nothing at all.

Part III will show you how to start your own mail drop, if this type of business is your cup of tea. You'll see the different approaches to starting up your small business, and the procedures you must follow to operate it. It will also lay out some of the pitfalls inherent in the remailing business, both from the operator's and the client's views.

This second edition also includes more information regarding postal scams and how to use a mail drop to protect yourself from them. We'll also discuss personal security more extensively, and show how a mail drop can be an asset for anyone concerned about parcel and letter bombs. We'll also get into techniques private investigators use to track people, and how mail security can defeat these techniques. Also new in this edition are several appendices, providing lists of mail drop operators, secretarial services, and private vaults you can use to enhance your secrecy and security.

Finally, this book is a complete resources handbook for anyone seeking to enhance his postal secrecy, and who is interested in methods to do so and the techniques that the "opposition" may use to track him down.

Notes:

1. Interview with Michael Kuzma, former manager of the now-defunct M.K. & Associates, a remail service.

Introduction
to Part I

What choices do you have in seeking mail privacy and convenience? There are many, as well as numerous reasons for seeking them. We'll examine several motivations to present an overview, and then look closely at various means, such as mail drops and post office boxes. You'll find that the choices are wider than commonly known, and that it's not necessary to do anything illegal to make your communications secure.

Chapter One:
Our Eroding Right To Privacy

One of the awkward aspects of living in a small town is that everyone knows everyone else's business. This can be stifling, especially if the mood of the populace is that nonconformism is akin to criminality.

The twentieth century has seen great efforts to enhance privacy, and one of the major changes has been the rise of the metropolis, filled with strangers who follow the credo of "mind your own business." However, there are certain government officials who feel that privacy is not so much a right as a cloak for criminal or subversive activities. These are the ones who feel that intensive surveillance of all citizens is essential for an orderly society. "Orderly" means according to their idea of "order."

Despite the passing of laws such as the Federal Privacy Act, our privacy becomes more vulnerable with each passing day. New technology provides professional snoopers more sophisticated means of penetrating into our affairs. Our mail is a good example.

The Mail Cover

A little known surveillance technique is the "mail cover." It takes a court order to open first-class mail, but this isn't necessary to set up a mail cover. The mail cover is an informal process whereby the mail carrier notes down the return addresses on mail delivered to the address under investigation. In one sense, this is worse than a court-ordered opening of the mail, because it's both covert and indiscriminate. Anyone who sends letter or package to an address under surveillance can wind up on a list of suspects. Postal Inspectors run mail covers for their own investigations, and in cooperation with other investigative agencies.

The most unpleasant aspect of this sort of investigation is the assumption of "guilt by association" on the part of the investigators. Because money-laundering operations, for example, often involve people with no criminal records, police agents are more ready to believe in the guilt of anyone who corresponds with suspects. Likewise, in their investigations of extremists, police agents are constantly seeking to widen the sphere of the investigation by enlarging the suspect list.

The advent of the computer has made surveillance easier. There are now "address bars" on envelopes, as businesses and even individuals obtain the equipment to make computerized mail sorting easier. Several programs for home computers print these bar codes along with the printed address. This also makes it much quicker to sort out suspect mail for special treatment. When all but a small minority print bar codes on their mail, the Postal Service will be able to make them mandatory, refusing to deliver any envelopes lacking these computerized addresses.

Routine opening of mail has been practiced by the Internal Revenue Service, the FBI, and the CIA, in various efforts to detect tax evaders, subversives, and other assorted individuals. One technique is "misdirected" mail, which "accidentally" goes to an IRS office, where employees open it and belatedly find out that it's not for them. They reseal it and send it on its way.[1]

Self-Defense Against Mail Surveillance

There are several defenses against this nefarious practice because there are several types of threats. One simple defense against a mail cover is simply not to have a return address on the envelope. This will work until the time that the Postal Service announces that it will no longer accept mail without a return address.

Preventing surreptitious reading of mail is somewhat more difficult. There are spray cans of solvents, such as cleaning fluid, (carbon tetrachloride, trichlorethylene, and perchloroethylene), which make some paper envelopes temporarily translucent, enabling a surveillance technician to read the contents. There are also ways of opening envelopes or removing the mail without opening the envelope. One way is by using a device resembling a knitting needle with a long cut separating it into two halves. Slipping this under the flap and onto the paper inside allows rolling up the letter and withdrawing it through the gap.

"Steaming" an envelope open allows resealing it while leaving minimal traces of the surreptitious entry. Using carbon tetrachloride to remove sealing tape is another method.[2]

There are several countermeasures to mail opening. One is to use "security envelopes" which have a dense printed pattern inside to prevent reading the letter through the envelope. Although chemicals may make the paper transparent, the inked pattern remains opaque, thereby preventing an inspector from reading the contents. Another step is to double-seal the envelope with Scotch tape. There are ways of removing this tape with solvents, and a precautionary step of sealing the flap with super glue will make it much tougher to open the envelope.

A neat way of deterring examination of the mail is by compounding the examiner's problems. Using several envelopes, one inside the other, will make it so difficult that he probably won't even try.

When using only one envelope, you can absolutely prevent reading of the contents through the paper by wrapping the letter in aluminum foil. This makes it impossible to read with any chemical spray without opening the envelope. Wrapping the letter in carbon paper will also provide security and prevent reading, and the pigment in the carbon paper will run if exposed to solvents. This alerts the addressee that someone has tampered with the contents. Using a marking pen to write across the sealing tape makes it very difficult to remove the tape and to replace it properly. The marking pen ink will run when exposed to solvents.

Another way to make it impossible to use any solvents without leaving a trace is to use several different types of ink to write the letter and address the envelope. Using a felt-tip for the return address and a ball-point for the address means that one or the other ink will run if sprayed with solvent. The sender can write the letter using several other pens, just to complicate the problem.

Avoiding examination is better than defeating it. This is why secret addresses have their place. A letter addressed to a fictitious identity at an address not under surveillance will escape scrutiny. This is where mail drops are useful.

Notes:

1. "Misdirected Mail," *Insight*, October 13, 1986.
2. Harrison, John, *CIA Flaps and Seals Manual*, 1975. This book is the best commonly available source dealing with surreptitious examination of mail. This 52-page manual is a complete guide to opening mail and resealing it without detection.

Chapter Two:
Why People Use Mail Drops

There are many reasons why people use postal boxes and mail drops. These have to do with convenience, personal security, and secrecy.

Nomads

People on the move, such as retirees, RV nomads, truck drivers, and merchant seamen, often have no fixed address or are away from home so much of the time that it's impractical to use a home address. Some will want their mail forwarded to various points where they may pick it up. For this, a remailing service is ideal.[1]

The nomadic lifestyle appears to have become increasingly appealing to retirees during the last part of the twentieth century. One source estimated that there were about 200,000 seniors who had sold their homes and decided to live on the road.[2]

Some stay for months at a particular RV park, while others keep moving. Some follow a seasonal pattern, emigrating south during the winter months, and returning to northern states to escape the summer's heat.

Most have had to sell their homes and property to pay for motor homes, which can be very pricey. Phone bills are high, as these nomads keep in touch with friends and families across the country, and there are fees for mail-forwarding services. While in theory any commercial mail drop will do, some mail drops have specialized in meeting the needs of nomads.

One remailing and forwarding service operating in the Western United States and specializing in nomadic clients is:

Snowbird Mail Service
3468 Vista Grande
Carson City, NV 89705
Telephone: (800) 828-9088

One RV-users association that provides a mail-forwarding service is:

Good Sam Club
64 Inverness Drive East
Englewood, CO 80112-5114
Telephone: (800) 234-3450
(303) 792-7284

This club is for people on the road, and offers a variety of services to those living the nomadic lifestyle. Among these services are emergency road service, various insurance plans, car rental and fuel discounts, and, most relevant to us, a mail-forwarding service. This is for club members, the only charge being for the postage needed to forward the mail. This comes to $45 per quarter for first-class mail, and the club requires advance payment. Charges will increase as postage stamps become more expensive.

One limitation is that this service is only for personal mail, not business mail. Also excluded are fourth-class books and tapes. A six-page brochure available from the club lays out conditions of service.

There is also a telephone message service at an additional charge. An 800-number makes it convenient for people leaving messages for you.

Another is:

Escapees, Inc.
100 Rainbow Drive
Livingston, TX 77351
Telephone: (409) 327-8873
(800) 9-ROVERS

Escapees began in 1978, advertises itself as a support network for RVers, and was incorporated in 1986. The group offers rallies, campgrounds in many western and southern states, emergency road services, an AT&T calling card, and a variety of other services.

The Escapees mail- and voice-message service has an 800 line for all subscribers, and allows members to choose a forwarding schedule which is convenient for them. The service also forwards packages, and accepts voice mail. Mail may be forwarded to any address the subscriber specifies, but Escapees warns that not all RV parks and campgrounds accept mail for guests.[3]

Personal Security

Some people have had mail stolen from their residential mail boxes. A locale with a high rate of residential mailbox thefts results in a high demand for post office boxes or mail drops. Postal fraud is another reason for not receiving mail at home or at a postal mailbox.

A popular scam reported in various areas of the country is for an outsider to file a change of address card on your home address, diverting your mail so that thieves can steal checks and other high-value items that come by mail. The scam artists are also after your credit card and bank mailings, from which they can glean your credit card numbers and expiration dates, using these to order merchandise by telephone. One victim was a physician at the Mayo Clinic, in Rochester, Minnesota, who noticed that her issues of *The New England Journal of Medicine* were no longer arriving. Scam artists had filed a change of address card in her name with her local post office, diverting her mail to an address in Brooklyn, NY. With her bank statements in hand, the gang had forged her name to documents and depleted her bank account.

Change of address cards, obtainable in 40,000 post offices across the country, are the key to this scam. Under post office rules, all that's necessary is to mail in the card to divert a person's mail to another address. Controls are nonexistent, demonstrated by the fact that the physician's name was not even spelled correctly on the card. One postal official has guessed that about 1,000 addresses a year are changed fraudulently.[4]

The normal procedure for post office employees to follow when receiving a change of address card is to send a change of address kit, consisting of notification cards for correspondents, to the new address. This does alert the person who has not moved, and whose address has been changed fraudulently. A new procedure the post office is testing in limited areas during early 1996 is to send a letter acknowledging the change of address both to the person's old address and the new one. This will alert the person if the change of address order is spurious. There may be other measures to increase security in the future.

Using a private mail service provides absolute protection against the change of address card scam, because postal regulations do not allow filing address change cards on individual clients using a mail drop. The post office bundles the mail to the "receiving agent" and will not filter out mail addressed to a particular individual.

Even with a private mail drop, fraud artists lay traps for the unwary. The following letter arrived at the author's private mail box, addressed to the "President" of the company. A call to the security manager of the author's bank revealed that providing account information can lead to the Nigerian scam artists' "vacuum-cleaning" all bank accounts by means of phony wire transfers, forged checks with account numbers electronically imprinted, and forged letters.

Similar letters have been received by others across the country, as this scheme is very widespread. Names on the letters vary, and it's a safe assumption that all are aliases. All letters promise quick money if the recipient provides his bank account numbers. Some claim that the money comes from petroleum companies' excess purchases, while others claim that an excess of import duties has created a fund to transfer out of Nigeria.

The surprising point about all of these letters is that they entice the recipient into a deal that is obviously shady. In this regard, it appeals to those with larcenous tendencies. A task force of Postal Inspectors, U.S. Secret Service Agents, U.S. Customs Agents, and Immigration and Naturalization Service Agents has been investigating these multi-million-dollar frauds, and recently a Nigerian received a 2½-year prison sentence for his role in promoting scams. Charles Nnabuife pleaded guilty in Atlanta Federal District Court, and Judge J.

Owen Forrester sentenced him to prison, and deportation upon his release, for mail and Social Security fraud.[5]

The Nigerian mail-fraud scam has even found its way into modern Russia. Peter Ford, a *Christian Science Monitor* staffer living in Moscow, found such a letter in his mail. Other tenants in his apartment building had received similar letters. Ford followed up, sensing a story. He invented a fictitious bank, bank account, and name, and sent this bogus information to the Nigerian fax number as directed in the letter. He received an immediate reply, telling him that he had to apply for a Nigerian contractor's certificate and a certificate of incorporation in Nigeria, at a cost of $11,600.[6]

Providing a checking account number is particularly dangerous. Unlike with a credit card account, there's no federal law limiting your liability. Bandits can vacuum-clean your account thoroughly, and you're very likely to find yourself stuck. The method used is the "demand draft," a little-known method of payment established by banks to allow withdrawals without your signature. This is like a check without a signature, and is normally used for automatic payment of mortgage payments and the like.[7]

The demand draft is particularly vulnerable to abuse. Its normal use is to cover mortgage payments, insurance premiums, club dues, and other periodic expenses, to save the account holder from having to sign individually for each payment. A serious problem often occurs when you decide to discontinue the service. On-line computer services have become notorious for ignoring the customer's request for cancellation and continuing to withdraw monthly payments from his account.

DR. JOE UDAH
TEL/FAX - 234 - 90 - 403181
LAGOS - NIGERIA

1ST MARCH, 1996

REQUEST FOR URGENT BUSINESS RELATIONSHIP

I am making this contact with you on behalf of my colleagues after a satisfactory information we gathered from an International Business Directory.

My colleagues and I are members of the Contract Award Committee (CAC) of the Nigerian National Petroleum Corporation (NNPC). I have been mandated by my colleagues to look for a trustworthy company into whose account some funds is to be transferred. The funds in question is $35.5M (Thirty-five Million, Five Hundred Thousand U.S. Dollars) now in a dedicated account with the Central Bank of Nigeria (CBN).

The above funds arose from the over-invoicing of some Supplies and Engineering Works contracts which have been executed and the contractors paid in full. The fund is therefore free to be transferred overseas without any risk whatsoever.

Due to the nature of acrual of this funds, it has to be applied for by a foreign contractor/company and payment can only be made into a foreign account hence this contact is necessary to accomplish this deal. You (or your company) shall be compensated with 30% of the amount as the account owner, 5% shall be used for the reimbursement of all expenses that will be incurred by either parties during the course of this financial transaction. The remaining 65% is for us.

We shall require of you the following urgently by fax:

1. Name of the Beneficiary
2. Name and full address of the company
3. Complete particulars of the Bank Account where you wish the funds be transferred. This should include the account number, bank address, the telephone, fax and telex numbers of the bank.

I and my colleagues have had some fruitful discussions with relevant top officials of both the Federal Ministry of Finance (FMF) and the Central Bank of Nigeria (CBN) and they have agreed to cooperate in the transfer.

An application for funds transfer shall be made at the appropriate Ministries in favour of the beneficiary (you or your company). Thereafter, your company shall be officially regarded as having executed the contract for the Nigerian National Petroleum Corporation (NNPC) for which payment is being made.

Please treat this transaction as **STRICTLY CONFIDENTIAL** as we are civil servants who would not want any exposure. Do not go through the International Telephone Operator (or AT & T) when lines are busy. Always dial direct.

Thanks for your anticipated co-operation.

Best regards.

DR. JOE UDAH

Letter sent by Nigerian scam artist to author.

The major problem with demand drafts is that they're very insecure, because the bank assumes that if the payee has the

customer's account number, the customer must have authorized it. A bank receiving a demand draft on a client's account from another bank won't even question it, any more than the post office challenges change of address notices.

The Federal Trade Commission has implemented new rules to reduce demand-draft abuses by telemarketers, following with a civil action against firms that abused them.[8] However, civil actions won't stop overt fraud rings that solicit your account numbers with get-rich-quick letters, such as the ones sent by Nigerian fraud artists.

A party to a divorce may seek mail privacy. A wife who has been the victim of domestic violence might have a real fear of her husband locating her while the divorce is in process. In other instances when child custody is an issue, one or the other party may want to keep the home address secret.

Public figures, including media people, have good reason to keep their home addresses secret. A series of phone calls and a threatening letter were the precursors to the killing of TV anchorwoman Diane Newton King in Battle Creek, Michigan, in February, 1991. Harassing phone calls and threatening letters are so common in the industry that they're nicknamed *Play Misty*-type calls and letters, after the Clint Eastwood movie.[9]

A celebrity, such as a national network anchor, has utility and credit card bills sent to his office or accountant. Another precaution is to receive personal mail at the office, although family members may choose a mail drop for their security.

Bombs in the mail arrive regularly. Mail boxes ranked 1st in the list of targets compiled by the Bureau of Alcohol, Tobacco, and Firearms for the years 1990-1994. Residences came in 2nd.[10] Post office employees are concerned about the increasing number of mail bombs sent, and one postal inspector puts the blame on publicity. Publicizing bombing incidents, he says, inspires copycats.[11] If you're expecting bombs in the mail, it's better to have them arrive at a mail drop than at your home.

Members of correspondence clubs of various sorts tend to use mail boxes or mail drops for secrecy. This is especially true of sexually oriented clubs, and some fringe political groups. Some use aliases, or simply list themselves as "Boxholder" in their ads, partly because their activities are stigmatized. Others simply are concerned about correspondents arriving on their doorsteps uninvited. See Chapter Nine for further information on this.

People who are heavily in debt might use mail drops to keep creditors at a distance. Others are seeking to enhance their financial privacy. See Chapter Five for a more detailed discussion.

Some people don't like to deal with the U.S. Postal Service for a variety of reasons. Despite an intensive public-relations campaign, the U.S. Postal Service has managed to offend a significant minority of citizens. The reason is that, despite all of the public-relations pabulum, the Postal Service and most of its employees don't care if they provide good service or not. The rules of the postal service make it almost impossible to fire an incompetent or uncaring employee, and this encourages even worse service.

Some people object to standing in lines. These folks seek small mail drops where their needs receive quick personal attention.

Those who are carrying on illicit correspondence with lovers, and who would suffer if family or friends discovered their covert relationships, may use mail drops.

Illicit radio stations, known as "pirate radio," use mail drops for security. An anonymous address protects the identities of pirate radio operators, who fear being "busted" by authorities.[12]

Yet another reason is tax avoidance. Some states, such as Nevada and Texas, have no state income tax, and establishing official residence in one of these absolves you from tax liability. A mailing address is a must for establishing such "residence."

Motor vehicle registration fees and insurance rates vary widely from state to state. States with lower registration fees are attractive, and a "residence" in a small town almost always produces lower insurance rates.

Businessmen

There are many uses for an untraceable or covert address in business, both from the employer's viewpoint and that of the employee. A secret address helps withhold the identity of the principal when feeling the way to open negotiations on sensitive issues.

Many businessmen like to get their mail early in the day. Collecting it from a box, post office or private, is quicker than waiting for mail delivery.

A small business starting out of someone's home or garage may benefit from a "prestige" address. Hiring a mail drop in a high-profile area can provide this. Using a foreign mail drop provides an address in another country, thereby opening several possibilities.

Mail drops in Switzerland and Liechtenstein provide prestige foreign addresses, with an aura of mystery and tax avoidance. However, there's also the possibility of abuse, as certain less-than-honest elements operate scams from foreign addresses.

A mail-order business run at home almost never uses the owner's street address. It's often more convenient to use a mail box or mail drop.

Some cities will not issue a business license to a business which is operated in a residential area, even if it's a very low-profile operation. A mail drop can provide the illusion of a business district address to satisfy the bureaucrats who issue the licenses.[13]

Another reason has to do with day-to-day security. Apart from wishing to safeguard themselves against possible embezzlement, employers often sort through the incoming mail to collect letters and other paperwork which they don't want any employees to see. One type of such paperwork might be bids. Another is acknowledgment of purchase orders placed by the purchasing department and returned by vendors. One company owner scrutinized these very carefully to see what his company was spending for materials and supplies. Scanning acknowledgments gave him the opportunity of canceling the order if he felt that it was unsuitable.

A businessman seeking to sell his company might advertise it in the classified section. If he lists his company's name or address, he may cause panic among his employees, and cause some to seek other employment. He'll also cause his customers concern. Having a box number instead of a street address is preferable in this case. A private mail drop provides the additional security of not being obliged to reveal the street address of a business box, as the Postal Service does upon demand.

An employer advertising for hired help might want to avoid having his lobby filled with applicants. This can be a serious problem in economically depressed areas where desperate job-seekers apply for anything and everything advertised. Listing only a box number without further identification, known as a "blind ad," keeps them at a distance. The employer can review the résumés and contact only the ones who interest him.

The employer also might want to keep his search secret from his employees. Many people are unwilling to believe that employers will lie brazenly to deceive those working for them. This is especially true during a business takeover, when the new employer will routinely state that he's not going to make any personnel changes. The new owner simply wants to forestall a mass exit by the staffers who are afraid of losing their jobs.

Even in individual cases, when the employer is seeking to replace someone, he doesn't want that person to quit before the employer has a replacement ready to step into that slot. With a box number, he can interview candidates and hire one secretly, bringing in the replacement at his convenience. At that point, he's also ready to deal with the incumbent.

A devious employer might run classified employment ads as a check on the loyalty of his employees. Although much of this is a pure waste of time, some obtain satisfaction from playing such games and ferreting out employees who are receptive to other employment opportunities.

Employees

An employee can also play games, only he has much more at stake. The employer might be concerned about one or two employees and their loyalty to him or their job performance. The employee has his livelihood and possibly his career at stake when seeking new employment, and discretion is often vital.

An employee seeking a change of employment might place an ad in the "Situations Wanted" section of a newspaper, using a box number for the address. This is often necessary because employers tend to view job-hunting by an employee with concern, and will in turn start seeking a replacement if they find out. Paternalistic employers look upon job-seeking by their employees as the gravest disloyalty, and will fire any such employee pre-emptively in reprisal as soon as they find out.

In each city and town, a few employers have developed bad reputations for this sort of behavior. Some are psychopaths who take it as a personal affront, and will fire on the spot anyone who gives notice. If you work for such a person, even a rumor that you're looking elsewhere can result in your losing your job. This is what makes job-seeking dangerous in some instances.

Anyone who announces an intention of seeking other employment out of misguided altruism, to allow his employer to find and train a replacement, makes himself very vulnerable. Even without malice, an employer will lay off anyone he knows to be seeking other employment if an order to cut back comes down the line.[14]

The other side of the coin is that an employee who has a grudge against another or who is trying to eliminate a dangerous competitor for promotion can take advantage of this sort of situation. He can place an ad in the "Situations Wanted" section in the other employee's name, listing his victim's home address. This is an attempt to "frame" that employee, and can be very effective if the boss is the vindictive type. It's only necessary to see to it that a copy of the ad lands on the boss's desk.

A job-seeker might also place a corresponding ad which reads like that of a potential employer in order to gauge the competition. Advertising the very type of job he's seeking will draw letters and résumés which will give him a good idea of who else is after that sort of job at the moment.

Applications

This quick sketch lays out some of the many reasons people have for seeking mail privacy. Some require more discussion, which we'll take up in following chapters.

Notes:

1. Peterson, Kay, *Home is Where You Park It*, Estes Park, CO, Roving Press Publications, 1982, pp. 157-161. Peterson suggests a remailing and message service specializing in the needs of wanderers.
2. Wilson, Craig, "RV Road Warriors; Retirees Turn To Full-time Traveling," *USA Today*, March 29, 1990, p. 1D.
3. "Be Sure Your Delivery Point Accepts Personal Mail," *Escapees*, January/February, 1996, p. 48.
4. McAllister, Bill, "Changes of Address Vulnerable to Fraud," *Seattle Times*, March 10, 1996.
5. Smothers, Ronald, "Nigerian Sentenced in International Fraud," *Seattle Times*, March 24, 1996, p. 16A.
6. Ford, Peter, "Russia is Now Rich Enough For Scams," *Christian Science Monitor*, March 11, 1996, pp. 1 & 8.
7. Willette, Annette, "Telemarkets Scams Tap Checking Accounts" *USA Today*, March 20, 1996, p. 1 A.
8. Crenshaw, Albert B., "Demand-draft Thieves Become Federal Target," *Seattle Times*, March 20, 1996, p. 2A.
9. Harney, James, "Everyone Suspect in TV Anchor's Killing," *USA Today*, February 12, 1991, p. 5A.
10. *Arson and Explosives Incidents Report*, 1994, Washington, DC, Department of the Treasury, Bureau of Alcohol, Tobacco, and Firearms, 1995, p. 21.
11. "Don't Open That Package!," *Time*, February 12, 1990, p. 20.

12. Horrvath, Robert, "North American Free Radio Directory," *Whole Earth Review*, Fall, 1990, p. 68.
13. Ives, Michael R., *The Mail Center Manual*, Huntington Beach, CA, 1980, p. 3
14. McGarvey, Robert, "Strategic Quitting," *Executive Female*, March-April, 1990, p. 34.

Chapter Three:
Post Office Boxes

Post office lock boxes are very popular as private, somewhat less-traceable addresses for individuals and businesses. The main use of a post office box is to mask the client's street address. A secondary use for a businessman is to keep incoming mail from his employees' eyes and reach until he's had the opportunity to screen it. The value of this is that he can remove all of the checks and close that avenue of embezzlement to potentially dishonest employees .

This doesn't always work. One small businessman who often traveled out of the country found that two of his employees conspired to raid his P.O. box while he was gone. The way they did this was to file a change of address order (Form 3575) on the postal box and have the mail forwarded to their home address. They had to forge their employer's name to do so, but the postal clerks routinely processed the order and duly forwarded the mail. The employees then deposited the checks in a bank account they'd established, as depositing individual and especially business checks attracts far less scrutiny than trying to cash them. When their boss returned, they had cleaned out the bank account and haven't been seen since.[1]

Businessmen who work from their homes may want a P.O. box. A mail-order operator, for example, may not want clients coming to his home. A post office box serves to conceal from clients the true premises from which the business operates.

Another use for a post office box is to support a "shell" business. A company listing itself as "Universal International Import-Export Industries" probably is, despite the imposing name, just a post office box and possibly a rented desk in an office. These facts are not immediately obvious to someone reading the address, although it doesn't take much "street smarts" to deduce the true status of the business. Shell businesses are useful for money laundering, "bust-outs," and other forms of frauds.

Postal employees can give out the street address of a business renting a box, but only if the boxholder has checked off the answer to question #4; "Will this box be used for soliciting or doing business with the public? Check one."

Obtaining a P.O. Office Box

Renting a post office box is fairly simple, requiring only filling out Form 1093, which is the application for the box, and paying the first term's rent. The postal employee who processes the form will require some form of I.D. from the applicant. This is usually a drivers license, or other photo I.D. A drivers license also serves to verify the client's address. If the I.D. doesn't show the address, other proof of address, such as an envelope mailed to the person at that address, must be shown.

CUSTOMER: Complete Items 1, 3-7, 15 and 19

(Item 2 for P.O. Use ONLY)

1. Name to which box number(s) is (are) assigned	2. Box/Caller Nos.
	Thru

3. Name of person making application *(If representing an organization, show title and name of organization if different from above)*

4. Will this box be used for soliciting or doing business with the public? *(Check one)*

a. ☐ Yes   b. ☐ No

5. Address *(No., Street, City, State and ZIP Code. Record address change on reverse and line out address below.)*	6. Telephone No. *(If any)*

APPLICANT PLEASE NOTE: Execution of this application signifies your agreement to comply with all postal rules relative to post office boxes and caller service.

7. Signature of applicant *(Same as Item 3)*	8. Date of application

ITEMS 8-14: TO BE COMPLETED BY POST OFFICE

9. Type of identification *(Driver's license, military identification, other; show identification no.)*	10. Eligibility for carrier-delivery ☐ CITY ☐ RURAL ☐ NONE	11. Box size needed

12. Dates of Service		13. Service Assigned	14. Information Verified by
a. Started	b. Ended	a. ☐ Post Office Box b. ☐ Caller c. ☐ Reserve Number	a. *(Initials)*

PS Form 1093, June 1993   (PART I) APPLICATION FOR POST OFFICE BOX OR CALLER SERVICE

Use separate card for each number or inclusive group of numbers, and type of service. File Part I alphabetically by Customer's Name.

CUSTOMER: Complete Items 15 and 19.

SPECIAL ORDERS	ITEMS 16-18: TO BE COMPLETED BY POST OFFICE
15. Postmaster: The following persons, or authorized representatives of the organizations listed are authorized to accept mail addressed to this (these) post office box or caller number(s). Continue on reverse if necessary. ☐ Check if reverse is used.	16. Post Office Box/Caller number for which this card is applicable _____ through _____ 17. ☐ Check if box is to be used for Express Mail reshipment.
a. Applicant *(Same as Item 3)*	18. Post Office Date Stamp
b. Name of box customer *(Same as Item 1)*	
c. Other	
d. Other	
CUSTOMER NOTE: Possession of post office box key or combination may be considered by the Postal Service to be valid evidence that possessor is authorized to remove mail from boxes.	19. I have read instructions and will comply
	Signature of Applicant *(Same as Item 3)*

PS Form 1093, June 1993   (PART II) APPLICATION FOR POST OFFICE BOX OR CALLER SERVICE

Use separate card for each number or inclusive group of numbers, and type of service. File Part II by box or caller number.

INSTRUCTIONS FOR WORKING COMBINATION BOX

1. Clear dial by three revolutions to the right, stop on ___ ___
2. Turn dial to the left and stop the second time around on ___ ___
3. Turn right and stop at ___ ___
4. Turn latch key LEFT to open

Your ZIP + 4 is: ☐☐☐☐☐ — ☐☐☐☐

Rules for use of Post Office Box and Caller Service

IMPORTANT: Post Office Box and Caller Service are Subject to the following and the regulations in Parts 951 and 952 DMM.

I. Mail, which is properly addressed to a post office box or caller service number, will be delivered through that post office box or caller service.

II. Customers must promptly notify correspondents of their current box or caller number address.

III. Post office box or caller service fees are paid in advance for one or two semiannual periods. A notice of fees due will be placed in a box or included with caller mail 20 days before the due date. If a boxholder is out of town and has submitted a temporary forwarding order, the notice will be mailed to the temporary address. It is the responsibility of the boxholder to assure that payment is made on time. If payment is sent by mail, it must be received by the postmaster by the due date. Payment may be by cash, or by check payable to the postmaster. Do not send cash by mail. If a check is returned by the bank, the box will be closed until that check is made good.

IV. If fee is not paid on time, the post office box will be secured so that mail cannot be removed through the door. If box or caller fees are not paid after 10 days, mail will be removed and treated as undeliverable, unless it can be forwarded in accordance with a change of address order. Closed post office boxes will be immediately available to new customers.

V. Post office boxes or caller service may not be used for any purpose prohibited by postal regulations. See Domestic Mail Manual (DMM).

VI. Boxes and caller numbers may not be used for the sole purpose of having the Postal Service forward or transfer mail to another address free of charge.

VII. Boxholders must promptly remove mail, or have it removed, from their boxes. Advance arrangements must be specifically made with the postmaster if mail is to be accumulated for more than 30 days and an overflow condition is probable.

VIII. Keys for key-type post office boxes will be issued upon payment of $1 for each key, including those initially issued for each post office

box. When a box is surrendered, all keys must be returned to the Postal Service. Fees for up to 2 keys will be returned to the boxholder. Keys for post office boxes may be obtained only from the Postal Service.

IX. Customers who use post office box or caller service, are required to maintain a current Form 1093, Application for Post Office Box or Caller Service, on file with the Postal Service. Any information on the application, which changes or becomes obsolete, must be corrected by promptly updating the Form 1093 on file with the postmaster at the office where the post office box or caller service is used.

X. Box or caller service may be terminated as provided in the DMM.
The customer may appeal a termination of service in writing to higher authority by following the detailed procedures in the DMM.

XI. Concerning information required for the completion of this form:
A. The collection of this information is authorized by 39 U.S.C. 403.404.
B. This information will be used to provide the applicant with post office box or caller service.
C. This information may be routinely disclosed:
1. To persons authorized by law to serve judicial process for the purpose of serving such process.
2. To a government agency, when necessary for the performance of its duties.
3. To anyone, when the box is being used for the purpose of doing or soliciting business to the public.
4. To a Congressional Office, at the request of the boxholder.
5. In response to a subpoena or court order.
6. Where pertinent to a legal proceeding in which the Postal Service is a party.
D. Completion of this form is voluntary; however, if this information is not provided, the applicant will be unable to use a box or receive caller service.

XII. Refer to the DMM for a more detailed explanation of these regulations.

PS Form 1093, June 1993 (PART III)

Postal Service Form 1093: Application for Post Office Box or Caller Service, Part III.

The Postal Service will release street addresses to any government agency requesting it. It may be a law enforcement agency, but also may be a welfare or Social Security agency. If you move, you may file a change of address order (Form 3575) to have the post office forward your mail to the address you direct.

Enhancing Secrecy

There are several ways of making a post office box work even better for you. One is to use false I.D. when you apply for the box. This is technically illegal, but nobody ever checks unless there's a criminal investigation by the postal inspectors. Another is to apply for a post office box some time before you move, and use your real I.D. This will mean that the post office will thereafter have an obsolete address for you. If you do not file a change of address form with them, there will be no official record of your move, and even a court order won't get this information out of the post office.

A third way, by far the most effective, is to use another person's box. The opportunities for this are more common than many people realize. If you have a friend or acquaintance whom you know has a box, and who is about to move out of the area, ask him for the key to his box when he leaves. It's no skin off his nose, and this provides a truly secret address for you. The only way for anyone to find you is to "stake out" the box, and if you pick up your mail infrequently or at irregular intervals this becomes expensive to do.

There are some drawbacks to this, though. For one, if you leave the key home one day, you can't ask the counter clerk for your mail. If ever you lose the key, you can't get another without showing I.D.

How P.O. Boxes Balance Out

As we'll see by comparing rates, P.O. boxes are far less costly than private mail drops. They're also far more secure and reliable, as far as the handling of your mail goes. The post office, however, won't forward your mail to your home or another address, won't receive UPS or other package shipments for you, and won't provide most of the other services that many private operators furnish as a matter of course. If you give up your box, however, you can file a change of address order and the post office will forward your mail to the address you specify. They will not do this for anyone who quits a mail drop, because this would require their sorting the mail drop's mail for individual addressees.

The post office usually has an unmanned lobby, open 24 hours a day. This offers access to boxes, as well as stamp machines, etc. The 24-hour access to the boxes is free, contrasted with the charge for a "lobby key" that some private mail drop operators impose.

Postal inspectors take an active interest in how their boxes are used, and are very aware that some sharp operators use them for fraud. This is why they scrutinize postal box clients carefully.

Notes:

1. The employer who was ripped off related this tale to the author in the post office one day.

Chapter Four:
What Can A Mail Drop Provide That A Postal Box Can't?

PLENTY! Let's list the possibilities briefly. Please note that not all mail drops are alike, and of course they won't all provide the same services. There is often an extra charge for extra services.

- Most don't have waiting lists for boxes, as do post offices in many locales. Obtaining a box is usually easier and quicker than renting one from the U.S. Postal Service, even if there are boxes available at the local post office.

- Many have street addresses, not post office box numbers. This avoids the "dead give-away" that a P.O. box involves. This also allows opening a "branch office" at the mail drop's location. Some firms open subsidiaries that are merely mail drops or secretarial services.[1]

- You can phone the mail drop to find out if any mail has come for you. Try this with your local post office. They won't tell you the time of day from your own watch.

- Mail drops are open longer hours than post offices. As a rule, mail drop operators and their employees are more

eager to please than the dull, rude, and catatonic post
office drones.[2]

♦ A mail drop will accept UPS, Federal Express, and other
private carrier packages for you, whereas a post office
won't. They usually do this without an extra charge,
either.

♦ A mail drop will also forward your incoming mail to any
address you specify. This usually involves an extra fee.
Any postage this requires will be extra because postal
regulation 153.212-c states that the delivery is complete
when the mail is delivered to the commercial agent. The
forwarding is with the express consent of the boxholder.
It's not likely to be the result of a dishonest employee's
slipping a forged address change order into the system, as
can happen with the post office.

♦ Mail-forwarding is especially valuable if you're on the
move a lot because you're a traveling salesman or a
retiree touring the country. You can instruct the mail drop
operator to forward your mail to specific points on your
itinerary where you can conveniently pick it up.

♦ A mail drop offers you privacy, as mail drop operators
keep your street address confidential. However, law
enforcement officers can obtain a court order to require
their cooperation.

♦ You don't always have to show I.D. when you rent a
private box, but need merely fill out Form 1583, which
the operator keeps on file. Usually, nobody checks this
out. At the post office, you must always show I.D. to rent
a box.

♦ Remailing is accepting a letter from a distant client, and
mailing it in that town or city to provide a local postmark.
The post office will not remail for anyone. This service is
very useful for someone trying to establish an address in
another locale.

♦ Remailing can also create the illusion that you're on vacation in a distant locale, by mailing picture postcards to friends and acquaintances at intervals.[3] This can be an extremely effective tactic for buying time and deterring or delaying a search for you.

♦ Remailing often includes shipping, which can be via the U.S. Postal Service, United Parcel Service, and other commercial carriers. Some mail drops will sell boxes and other packaging materials, and will even package the goods for the client. Note that those which accept parcels for shipment via UPS and other commercial carriers charge a premium for the convenience.

♦ Some offer secretarial services, including typing, photocopying, and notary service. This may also include word processing, quick printing, and business cards. Many mail drops today offer fax service.

♦ Some also arrange for telegrams and money orders. A mail drop with a Western Union service offers quick financial transactions.

♦ One mail drop offers a check service. This means a check drawn upon their account, which conceals the identity of the person making the payment. This is:

Budd's Remailing Service
R.R. #1, Box 63
Eldorado, Ontario, Canada KOK IYO
Phone: (613) 473-4838
Fax: (613) 473-4443

Budd provides international bank drafts, postal money orders, and a checking account in U.S. funds for those who want to make untraceable payments. The checking account is totally anonymous for the client, with no clue regarding who originated the payment.

- In some instances, a mail drop can also serve as an improvised safe deposit box. Mailing something to yourself at the mail drop is one way of keeping it "on ice" until you need it or the rent runs out. One remailer provides "safekeeping service" for regular clients, storing materials in a safe, for as long as the client wishes.[4]
- Some mail drops are run as a sideline to other businesses, such as locksmith shops and accounting services. This is why some offer unusual additional services such as key duplication, locksmithing, passport photos, rubber stamps and office supplies, and other miscellaneous services. In addition, some mail drops are franchises, with central supply and service arrangements to allow individual operators to offer more services than they would otherwise.

Florida's Loomis Drugs originally operated a postal substation, but now has converted it to a private service called the "Mailing Depot." This operation sells lottery tickets, office and packaging supplies, fax services, and keys. It also rents boxes and accepts UPS packages.[5]

- Mail drops offer a lot to the person who needs more than a mailing address. As we'll see, there are also other and more specialized services that are tailored to special needs.

Notes:

1. Budd, Wayne, *The Official Remailing Guide*, Eighth Edition, Eldorado, Ontario, Canada, 1993, pp.20-21.
2. Garrett, Echo Montgomery, "Mailbox Missionary: Anthony DeSio Takes on the Post Office," *Success*, March, 1990, v37, p. 62.

3. Budd, Wayne, *The Official Remailing Guide*, Eighth Edition, Eldorado, Ontario, Canada, 1993, p. 18.
4. *Ibid.*, p. 16.
5. "Mailing Centers Becoming Latest Traffic-building Strategy," *Drug Store News,* February 19, 1990, p. 52.

Chapter Five:
Financial Privacy

There's an increasing effort by the Internal Revenue Service to collect taxes. This is especially true in their surveillance of several "target groups," specifically self-employed persons earning income in the fifty to one hundred thousand dollar bracket.

One way to obtain financial privacy is to open a savings or checking account with an out-of-state bank using a mail drop in the bank's locale.[1] Some banks have "bank by mail" services. Looking through telephone directories for the locations of your choice is a quick and easy way to build up a list of addresses. Writing to both mail drops and banks in the area will soon provide a list of firms which will cooperate with you in your needs.

American investors are strictly limited by U.S. laws regarding what they may send overseas, and even the information they may receive from off-shore banks and businesses. There are international agreements limiting the amounts of funds Americans may have in overseas banks. One way of getting around this is to hire a remailing service in another country and use its address as a base for foreign investments.[2]

Laundering Money

"Laundering" money is usually a crime, because it's linked with an effort to evade taxes or to conceal the source of criminally derived assets. With the advent of the "RICO" (Racketeer Influenced and Corrupt Organizations) laws, both the federal and state governments are seizing not only contraband, but the proceeds of drug dealing, illegal gambling, and other vices for profit.

The mail drop serves a vital role in money laundering on a budget. It's a convenient and relatively inexpensive way to provide a dummy "company" to generate paperwork to cover an illicit transaction. One way to launder money is to have it surface as "legitimate" income. You then have to pay taxes on it, but you conceal its criminal origins. An example of this is the vending machine ploy.[3]

The money launderer begins by buying a number of vending machines. Vending machines sell everything from pantyhose to cigarettes and condoms. Condoms are a good bet right now because of the AIDS scare, and IRS investigators will find it harder to establish "norms" for sales volume. The basic technique in laundering money through vending machines is to have the sales records match the amount of money to be laundered. To cover this, it's necessary to buy an amount of product that coincides with the sales figures. Doing this means sacrificing a lot of money for useless stock, however. Making the operation more profitable means recycling stock, and this is where a mail drop serves the purpose.

The first step is to set up a false "wholesaler" in another city, establish an address, and have stationery and invoices printed. The vending machine company buys stock from the "wholesaler" to cover the alleged retail income. The theme of the scheme is that the launderer sells the merchandise back to himself. The stock need not physically move from one place to another, although having warehouse and shipping records will help substantiate the operation if there ever is an investigation. This ploy works for a variety of merchandise, including videotapes and other goods which sell both over-the-counter and mail-order.

The Dummy Company

An important point about forming a dummy company, or "shell corporation," is that it's convenient to have more than just a mail drop. The Yellow Pages contain listings under "Secretarial Services" for a more comprehensive operation. A secretarial service can provide a mailing address, office space, a telephone number and a live receptionist to answer it, as well as taking care of paper processing such as posting invoices and making out other paperwork. A business letterhead printed to substantiate the company's existence helps. This is more expensive than a simple "mail drop," but for the purpose it's worth it. More expensive yet is renting an office and hiring a receptionist. If there are large amounts of money at stake, paying the freight for a class act is worthwhile. We'll cover secretarial services and other choices more thoroughly later.

Notes:

1. Interview with Michael Kuzma, former manager of the now-defunct M.K. & Associates, a remail service.

2. Budd, Wayne, *Official Remailing Guide*, Eighth Edition, Eldorado, Ontario, Canada, 1993, p. 4.
3. Gregg, John, *How to Launder Money*, Port Townsend, WA, Loompanics Unlimited, 1982, pp. 42-43.

Chapter Six:
Private Storage Facilities

There are several types of private storage facilities available. One is the private storage room, available from an operator who offers rooms varying in size for different needs. Another is the private safe deposit box, which has become popular during the last few years.

The reason for this increase in popularity is that a bank safe deposit box is subject to rules issued by the Treasury Department. The Internal Revenue Service, always seeking hidden assets, has a little trick to induce you to reveal your safe deposit box: the annual fee is tax-deductible. By deducting the fee, you inform the IRS that you have a bank safe deposit box.

There are also state laws. Some states, for example, require that a bank officer send an inventory of a deceased box-holder's contents to the state tax authority. Most of these rules are to make it easier for the Internal Revenue Service and other agencies to collect taxes by tracing and confiscating undeclared assets.

Private storage operators are not subject to the banking laws, and are in a better position to maintain secrecy. At the moment, private vault fees are not deductible as such, but if ever they become so, it would be a major mistake to list this on any tax return.

Clients may simply be people who value their privacy. They may also be active in the underground economy. There are also forbidden collectibles such as gold bullion and other valuables which the government sees fit to control or ban from time to time. Some keep firearms and ammunition stored against the prospect of a nationwide gun confiscation law.

Another type of client is the "survivalist." This client is interested in securing some valuables from nuclear attack, or other invasion or catastrophe, and chooses a private vault, some of which are built into the sides of mountains or buried underground. Some are in remote or semi-remote areas on the assumption that nuclear bombs are less likely to drop there.

Clients of private vaults are not just individuals. Corporations intent on preserving their records in the event of nuclear war or other catastrophes have had them microfilmed, and stored the films in these vaults.

A comprehensive list of private vaults appears in Appendix II.

Private storage operators are not necessarily in the business of mail receiving, but also operate mail drops on their premises. If the private vault you hire near you doesn't offer this, it may be possible to work out a deal with him. An extra payment is almost always the best way to persuade an operator to provide the extra service. This can include receiving mail or packages and keeping them for the owner. Because the operator always has a master key, he can gain access to the storage rooms and place the packages inside. If the rooms are fitted with hasps for padlocks or combination locks, providing the operator with an extra key or with the combination will allow him entry. This places a lot of reliance on his integrity, however.

The private vault is for material which you can't keep at home or in a bank, and which requires very secure "burial." You can expect to pay a premium for this privacy.

Chapter Seven: Electronic Mail Drops

Conventional mail drops serve a good purpose, but they're slow because of the time it takes to send the paper. There are quicker means of communication.

Unlisted Telephone Numbers

There are several types of "unlisted" numbers available, at extra cost, from the telephone companies in most parts of the country. One type merely lists your name and number in the directory, omitting your street address. Another omits your listing completely, and it's not available from Directory Assistance.

Any unlisted number is available to police officers, and private investigators have ways of obtaining them as well, which we'll discuss in Chapter Fifteen. There is one way to obtain a telephone number without having your name appear attached to it in any telephone company records. This requires a little luck, specifically encountering a telephone which you can take over from the previous party. If you're renting, for example, the previous renter may not have had his telephone service transferred, and if you keep paying the bill, you'll have use of a telephone which is not in your name at all.

The way to keep it really under cover is, of course, to pay via money order under the old name, not by your personal check. This method totally avoids leaving your name in any telephone company's business office, where a persistent investigator might discover it. However, be warned that there exist other ways of discovering your secret telephone number, and many investigators know all of the tricks.

Call Forwarding

The telephone company, never missing an opportunity to make money, now offers two services which function as electronic mail drops. "Call forwarding" simply means that you can have any calls coming to your phone automatically switched to another telephone. The caller dials a number and thinks that the party who answers is actually at that number. This is very useful for maintaining the illusion of an address in the business district while answering the telephone at home. A telephone number rented from a "secretarial service" serves as the listed number.

"Remote call forwarding" is even better. There are "Wide Area Telephone Service" (WATS) lines available, but they all have an 800 prefix in place of the area code. Any telephone user knows that they are not geographically linked. With remote call forwarding, it's possible to rent an empty office or a line from a secretarial service and foster the illusion that it's manned. The caller dials the number with the area code, unaware that the person answering may be many hundreds of miles away.[1]

The Answering Service

Both call forwarding and remote call forwarding require that you have telephone service, under your name or an alias. So does the conventional answering service, which ties in to your own phone. An operator "picks up" on the third or fourth ring if you don't answer. The operator may answer with your name, as in "Mr. Jones' office," or if you instruct her to do so, she may simply say "Good afternoon, 1443," answering only with the last four digits of the number.

The Answering Machine

If you're simply seeking to screen out nuisance calls, such as telemarketers, an answering service will do very well. A less expensive method is to install a telephone answering machine and never to answer the phone directly. The outgoing message on the machine says:

> *"This is John Jones. Thank you for calling. I can't come to the phone right now, but if you'll please leave your name and number I'll get back to you as soon as I can."*

If you're home, you can hear who's calling you with the monitor speaker on. You can immediately interrupt the machine by turning it off and answering the call yourself. Most modern answering machines have a switch that immediately turns off the recorder when it senses that someone has picked up the handset. If the caller is someone you don't want bothering you, such as a salesman, you can simply ignore the call. Most salesmen hang up instantly if they reach an answering machine, as hardly anyone ever calls them back.

You can combine the answering machine with a "Caller ID" box for more convenience. The Caller ID box displays the number calling you, and you can decide whether to answer the phone even before the answering machine kicks in to take the call. However, the limitation is that unlisted numbers will not display. Neither will "blocked calls," in which the caller presses a code (usually *67) into the keypad when he makes his call, to avoid letting the party he's calling know who he is. If the caller doesn't want you to know who he is, let the answering machine take the call.

The Electronic Message Drop

The other type of answering service does not tie in to your line, but simply takes messages. This is less expensive, and is usually an auxiliary service offered by a mail drop or secretarial service. You call in at intervals to get the messages and return the calls you wish. Consider it an electronic message drop.

Paging

Finally, there is the paging service. This requires that you carry a pager with you to receive a page. There are several types of pages.

The first is simply a beep-beep tone to tell you that there's a message waiting for you. When you hear the tone, you phone in for your message. For covert use, one model vibrates instead of beeping, to avoid alerting anyone nearby that you're carrying a pager.

Another, more sophisticated type of paging service issues a pager which displays the number you are to call. These are very common today.

Yet another type has a small speaker. Anyone dialing your page number gets through to you directly, for one-way communication. This may be convenient in one sense, but can also be a hassle. If the person trying to contact you doesn't speak clearly, you may not understand his message. A high noise level around you may interfere with hearing him. With one-way communication, you have no way of asking for a repeat. If you're with someone, this person can overhear the message, which could be embarrassing or inconvenient for you. Yet another disadvantage is that this is the most costly type of service.

Notes:

1. Gregg, John, *How to Launder Money*, Port Townsend, WA, Loompanics Unlimited, 1982, pp. 34-35.

Chapter Eight
The Secretarial Service

Using A High-End Service

Secretarial services are not mail drops. A bare-bones secretarial service offers dictation and typing. Almost all have found it profitable to offer more than these services because the demand exists.

The Instant Office

For the businessman in a strange town who needs the facilities of an office, the secretarial service can provide almost everything he might wish, a true office away from home. As a start, there is dictation and typing. A message service is another prospect, for the executive on the go who needs a home base and message center. Some secretarial services have offices and conference rooms for rent on a daily basis, for those who need such comprehensive facilities.

Other related services are usually available. These include photocopying, cassette transcriptions, telex and fax, mass mailing (including labels and envelopes), and cover letters. Some offer a telephone-answering and message service, taking calls for you when you're not there.

On a higher plane, there are specialists in writing reports, résumés, theses, word processing, editing, legal manuscripts, and newsletters. All of these can make life easier for the uprooted businessman. Other services can include temporary help, such as a "Girl Friday," travel arrangements, pickup and delivery, bookkeeping, and of course, assorted mailing services.

There are two very good aspects regarding secretarial services compared with mailing services. One is that they don't expect the customer to fill out Form 1583 and show I.D. Secretarial services are not mail drops in the sense that that is not their primary business. Because of this, they've slipped through the cracks in the legislative floor and are not hassled by the postal inspectors.

The main point regarding hiring a secretarial service is to make a good initial impression. The "power suit" and company-size checkbook in a Mark Cross briefcase combine to project a good image. Having a few letterheads to reinforce the impression can only help, especially when you have one of the typists do a letter on one.

The cost for receiving mail there is higher, in the $30-per-month bracket, but there's usually a prestige address that goes with it and no need to put a box number or a "suite" number on the address. For this kind of money, the staff of the secretarial service takes extra care and sorts the mail by name.

The secretarial service offers the chance to set up an instant dummy corporation or "branch office," if desired. The borrowed address, premises, and equipment mean that a full-blown operation can be set in motion on short notice, and just as quickly dismantled. This is a higher-class operation than possible by any other means except actually renting an office and hiring a staff. A comprehensive list of secretarial services in the 50 largest U.S. cities is in Appendix III.

Chapter Nine:
Using Mail Drops For Sex

Mail drops figure prominently in any sort of sex-by-mail operation. There are several reasons for this. The person who engages a mail drop may want to keep his activities secret from family and friends. A mail drop also helps to conceal identity, which is some protection against blackmail. Some types of sex-linked activities, such as buying and selling "kiddie porn," are downright illegal, and carry heavy penalties.

Sexually Explicit Materials

In many communities, pornography is considered depraved, and anyone who has a reputation to protect, such as a businessman or member of the clergy, will want to avoid revealing this interest. A home delivery with a torn envelope that reveals the contents can be very compromising. Postal employees, who handle thousands of pieces of mail each day, develop a skill at recognizing porn, especially because it usually comes in a "plain brown wrapper." In some instances, postal workers who recognize the source of the material may "accidentally on purpose" tear the envelope out of malice.

Another danger when ordering certain pornographic materials from abroad is from the federal authorities. The U.S. Customs Service regularly spot-checks ads with foreign addresses in American publications, and compiles lists of those who order from them. There are "target lists" of people who order sexually oriented materials from overseas.[1] Some of these lead to criminal prosecutions .

Child Pornography

Title 18, Section 2252, U.S. Code, deals with the sexual exploitation of minors. For the purposes of this section, a "minor" is anyone under 16 years of age. This is the well-known "kiddie porn" statute, and it bans producing, buying or selling child pornography for the purpose of resale. The U.S. Customs Service opens about 270,000 pieces of mail per year in its search for "contraband."[2] Contraband can mean illegal drugs, imports on which Customs can collect import duties, and items illegal to mail or ship without a special permit, such as firearms, ammunition, and explosives.

Those who order "kiddie porn" from overseas can have their materials confiscated. The U.S. Customs Service will seize it and notify the addressee of the action, and offer him the opportunity to make a court appearance to show cause why the material should not be confiscated.

In addition, law enforcement agents compile mailing lists of certain sexually oriented publications. This isn't difficult at all, because many such publications sell their mailing lists, which are in demand by other, similar, publications and purveyors of sex toys. Publications that don't sell lists are subject to mail covers. Another way is to place an undercover agent on the staff. Still another way is to exploit the arrest of any staff member, who may be arrested on a charge unrelated to his employment. An investigator can make the most of this by using the criminal charge to coerce that person's cooperation. .

Sex and "Swinger's" Clubs

Memberships in various sorts of sex clubs can also be embarrassing if they come to light. A letter opened accidentally by another family member can cause severe repercussions. In addition, some sex or "swinger" clubs provide each member with a copy of their membership lists. Such clubs aren't particular regarding whom they accept as members. Anyone with a mailing address and the fee gets a membership card and a copy of the list. Each membership renewal comes with an update of the list. A police officer or private investigator can subscribe, using a mail drop and an alias, and obtain a list of potential suspects.

Anyone who joins a sex club of any sort, or corresponds on sexual matters ("J/O Letters") has to cope with the possibility of running into some "flakes." Flakes are undesirable or even dangerous for one reason or another, and you certainly would not want one to show up on your doorstep. Some of these people spend their vacations traveling around the country on sexual tours, and a few will show up unannounced. This can be quite embarrassing, and is why many who advertise in sexually oriented publications use aliases and mail drop addresses.

Another reason is the possibility of blackmail or retaliation by "hate mail." In Chicago, in 1987, a person or group calling itself the "Great White Brotherhood of the Iron Fist" placed a spurious ad in a weekly newspaper that catered to sexually oriented traffic. The ad was aimed at homosexuals, and those who responded found that copies of their letters were being sent to their families, neighbors, landlords, and employers.

The possibility of embarrassment or harassment is a good reason for using an alias in any such correspondence. It's not absolute protection, but a false name, coupled with a false address, makes you harder to trace.

Some publications operate a sideline to the remailing industry, offering classified advertisers "box numbers" and a remail service. This has become almost standard practice because some people have placed phony ads in sexual publications, with the names and addresses of church-going fundamentalists, in order to embarrass them. Almost all such magazines use boxes for their own protection. The service generally works like this:

A paragraph at the beginning of the classified section advises readers that some of the ads are coded with box numbers instead of listing the individual's name and address. Those who reply to an ad must enclose their reply in a sealed and stamped envelope with the box number written in pencil, for ease of erasing. They must enclose this envelope inside a larger envelope addressed to the publication's classified ad department, including the forwarding fee, which is usually a dollar or two. The publication's staff will erase the box number and write the boxholder's address on the envelope.

Alternately, some publications use voice-mail service, including a 900 number which respondents may call. This protects anonymity, and provides the publication with another source of income.

It's hard to judge a service of this type. Because it's unreasonable to expect a reply from all of the ads answered, it's difficult to estimate how many are legitimate and how many have been placed by the magazine's staff to increase the number of remailing or 900-number fees earned.

The role of mail drops in various sexual activities is traditional, and probably won't decrease. Even legalization of all forms of sexual expression would not affect this significantly, because as long as people feel that they have something to hide, whatever the reason, mail drops will thrive.

Notes:

1. Interview with Michael Kuzma, former manager of the now-defunct M.K. & Associates, a remail service.
2. Smith, Robert Ellis, *Privacy: How to Protect What's Left of It*, Garden City, NY, Anchor Press/Doubleday, 1980, pp. 281-282.

Chapter Ten:
Law Enforcement And Mail Drops

Law enforcement officers use mail drops as return addresses to build up suspect lists for various categories of crimes. If the officer is a postal inspector, he'll probably use a post office box. However, for certain stings, postal inspectors have used street addresses abroad.

Using Mail Drops for
Sting and Intelligence Operations

The basic technique is to scan the tabloids, "swinger" publications, specialty erotic magazines, bikers' and dopers' magazines, and any others which contain ads that might pertain to an illegal activity. The officer writes a letter responding to the ad, and solicits whatever the person placing the ad is offering. The reply may be entered in evidence, or if it's not enough for a prosecution, serves as a stepping stone for another letter to obtain more information or evidence.

It's virtually certain that every sex-by-mail club in this country has had at least one applicant who was an undercover police officer or postal inspector. This is especially true of any that publish membership lists. Political fringe groups such as the "Posse Comitatus," which used to advertise for members via ads in paramilitary, mercenary, and survival magazines, are usually targets of law enforcement information-gathering.

The paramilitary magazines have classified ad sections which offer some unusual goods and services, among them murder-for-hire. *Soldier of Fortune* magazine ran a "Gun for Hire" ad placed by two men who were later arrested for contract murder. One client asked the killers to liquidate his wife and make it look like robbery, for a fee of $20,000.[1]

Another type of ad police watch carefully offers kits for making illegal weapons. These are very interesting to law enforcement officers, especially postal inspectors and officers of the Bureau of Alcohol, and Tobacco, and Firearms, also known as BATF. Anyone who advertises machine gun parts can expect a letter from a BATF agent posing as a purchaser. A person who places a murder-for-hire ad will receive letters from postal inspectors and other lawmen to find out exactly what he's offering.

If the investigation results in an arrest, there's always an accompanying confiscation of the seller's records, which include the names and addresses of people with whom he's dealt. This provides an excellent "suspect list" which the law officers can disseminate to local police agencies. Let's take a hypothetical instance, based upon a real-life happening, to illustrate how this works:

John Smith, of Mobile, Alabama, had thought of murdering his nagging wife. Concerned about the consequences, he answers an ad in *Shoot 'em Up* magazine for a contract killer. The letter he gets in reply tells him, in guarded language, that "special services" are available upon demand, and will be negotiated in person for each individual case. An agent will be available in his area on a certain date, and if Mr. Smith wants to meet with him for further information, he may call a certain telephone number for an appointment.

Smith never calls, unable to make a firm decision. Meanwhile Jones, who is seeking to get rid of his business partner, answers the ad and consummates a deal which results in his partner's quick and violent demise. The plan misfires, however, in the sense that both Jones and the contract killer are arrested for the murder. A search warrant results in Smith's name and address, along with many others, falling onto the hands of the investigators. A summary of the case goes to the police agency with jurisdiction of the area in which each person lives, as a lead in case someone known or related to the person has recently died violently. The local agencies review the information, trying to match up the names with any unsolved murders which have recently occurred.

Smith's name remains on file with the local police, along with the "case history" of the murder-for-hire organization. The practical consequences will be nothing for Smith, because it's not a crime to answer a classified ad. However, if his wife ever dies under suspicious circumstances, he'll be the focus of an investigation. Another possible consequence can result if Smith ever applies for a license in which the police have a discretionary power of refusal. For example, if the locale Smith is in requires a permit for a firearm, his application will go to the local police, who will review it in the light of the information attached to his name. The same goes for a liquor license, a private investigator's license, and other pieces of official paperwork that require police review before granting.

The search for mailing and membership lists is intense. Any police agent conducting surveillance on a political "extremist" organization and its members always seeks to obtain more suspects, because that's how the investigation proceeds and gathers momentum.

Any arrest will result in a search warrant for the arrestee's premises. Although the search warrant must specify the reason for the search and the type of material needed for evidence, a loophole allows the police an enormous amount of latitude.

The "exclusionary rule" states that illegally obtained evidence is "tainted" and may not be presented in prosecution. However, this applies only to evidence that shows up in court. During recent years, several court decisions have upheld evidence seized in "good faith" during the execution of a warrant. One loophole is the "plain view" doctrine, and another is that evidence in error may be admissible if the mistake is "reasonable."[2]

Investigative "leads" are not evidence, and never appear in court. This means that information-gathering of this sort can be free and easy.

In executing a search warrant, a mailing list is almost never sought as evidence. However, if there's one on the premises, there's nothing to prevent police agents from seeing it, copying it, and using it as information for developing additional leads.

It's a safe assumption that law enforcement officers make an extra effort to arrest members of organizations on police proscription lists in order to have excuses for search warrants. In some instances, the lifestyles and daily activities of these people provide adequate excuses for arrests. One excellent example is a weapons charge. Most people who carry concealed weapons for protection, but without a permit, are never stopped and frisked by police officers. If they're on a suspect list, they can expect to be stopped on a pretext and searched, in order to justify an arrest and the search warrant to follow.

In other instances, the police can use an informer as an *agent provocateur* to "plant" contraband and justify a search. To obtain a search warrant, it's necessary to present a judge with an affidavit listing the premises to be searched, the reason for the search, the type of evidence sought, and the reasons why the police believe that it will be found on the named premises. This procedure is easier in some locales than in others, because the police have a "friendly judge" on tap to sign a search warrant they desire. The "friendly judge" is not too exacting in reviewing search warrant affidavits, which makes it much easier for a police agent to obtain one on fabricated "probable cause."

Another type of information-gathering is attempting to rent mailing lists from various publications. Whatever the orientation of the magazine, the owner and operator is a businessman first, and often he'll rent his subscription list upon demand. This is standard practice in the publishing industry and exotic magazines are not necessarily exempt from this. In fact, there are very few exceptions.

This is undercover work on a very low level, with no personal contact with suspects or potential suspects. Its main value lies in the little investigative time it absorbs in proportion to the possible returns. The names go into a computer database. Adding names from other lists and other sources enables getting a "match" on some names. This allows law officers to build up "constellation" charts displaying the names most active in a particular field. Typically, these are not suspects, but only potential suspects. Still, the matching of names allows the law officers to focus their investigative activities more narrowly.

An example is the case of a child molestation. Officers may not have an identifiable suspect because of a lack of witnesses. They therefore have to work on lists of potential suspects, which can come from several sources.

One is a list of registered sex offenders, in states which require people who have ever been convicted of sex crimes to register with the police whenever they move. Another is a list of suspects in previous investigations of the same sort. This sometimes points a finger, as in the case of a molestation in a preschool where the same person had worked in a preschool where a similar case had occurred previously. It's another matter if the suspect has had no arrests or convictions for sexual offenses. The investigation must then be more widespread.

As with the instance of respondents to ads in vicarious violence magazines, the names of subscribers to sex magazines are disseminated to local police for matchups. The results vary with the local department. It may be only of academic interest to know that a pillar of the community subscribes to a "masturbation mag," but it can be crucial information if he also subscribes to "kiddie porn" and there's been a juvenile sex killing in the community.

Soliciting letters from subscribers to such magazines is one way of gathering evidence, or at least indicators that the persons may be interested in committing illegal acts. The detective pretends to have the same sexual interests as his targets, and offers to exchange stories of sexual acts with them. Experience has shown that some who answer ads in such magazines are extremely uninhibited in relating their exploits and fantasies. This may be because of the anonymity possible in these vicarious encounters, or more probably because they don't understand how it's possible to trace them and discover their true identities with almost 100 percent accuracy. This helps build up an active suspect list, and in some instances provides evidence of illegal acts the target has committed.

The Threads of Investigation

A typical case, as reported in *The Oregonian*, a Portland, Oregon, newspaper, and the *Arizona Republic*, is "Operation Looking Glass," run jointly by postal inspectors and local law enforcement officers. This case is worth describing in detail because it ties together the many threads of an investigation, and shows the variety of techniques and agencies that cooperate on a case. "Operation Looking Glass" got its name because of the alleged pedophilia of Charles Dodgson, the English mathematician and author who wrote *Through The Looking Glass* and *Alice's Adventures in Wonderland* under the pen name Lewis Carroll.

This case got its start in 1977, according to court documents, when Los Angeles County Sheriff deputies executed a search warrant on a home in Los Angeles, finding a customer list with 2,000 names. This provided an immediate "suspect list" for law officers in many jurisdictions, and had ramifications across the country. A second, but smaller, customer list turned up during a search of another porno producer in June, 1987.

Postal inspectors decided upon a "sting" operation. They opened up several "fronts" for the sale of child pornography. Ads also stated an interest in buying child pornography from clients. One of these stings, the "Far Eastern Trading Company," operated from a mail drop in the U.S. Virgin Islands. Some of the techniques used were advertisements in pedophile publications, such as *Loveland*, and direct-mail solicitation. This sting was "blown" and it was exposed as an undercover operation in the October 1986 issue of *Boy Love World*. There have been others operating without having been discovered.

Of course, postal inspectors don't use their home or office addresses and don't announce themselves as law officers in their ads. One postal inspector named "Calvin Comfort" used the alias of "Jolene Edwards" in pursuing a kiddie porn case. In soliciting pornographic materials, "Edwards" used a post office box instead of a street address. Post office boxes do well as mailing addresses for undercover operations because they're in common use by porno traffickers and dealers in sex toys.

According to one search warrant affidavit filed by a Phoenix, Arizona, Police Department detective in June, 1987, a batch of solicitation letters were mailed on March 20, 1987, to names on the original California list. One person used a post office box at a downtown Phoenix branch, and had appeared on the list under the name of "Mark Klarke." Also involved in the investigation of this person was correspondence with a postal inspector, David Wood, who used the alias "Richard Teninch" and a Las Vegas mail drop. This elicited what amounted to a written confession from "Klarke," who described alleged encounters with underage females and provided photocopies of written kiddie porn.

"Klarke" received a letter from the "Far Eastern Trading Company" and he responded, which resulted in a series of letters between him and the postal inspectors operating the sting. "Klarke" ordered two items of child pornography and also offered to sell material he had to "Far Eastern." The package containing his order arrived at the post office box with a small transmitter inside, which would send a signal when the package was opened.

Postal inspectors and Randy Wakefield, a prosecutor for the Maricopa County, Arizona, County Attorney's Office, revealed that there are over one hundred investigations underway as a result of the lists uncovered in California, and that there is an effort being made to identify the people on the lists. Although they were not specific regarding the methods used in identification, a database matchup is surely part of the process.

Because the material that "Klarke" provided to "Teninch" offered an opening for a prosecution, "Klarke" was prosecuted under an Arizona State law which prohibits sexual exploitation of minors.

Other Offenses

Mail frauds and extortion letters are the province of the postal inspectors. Postal inspectors regularly use postal boxes and mail drops to secure evidence against fraud artists who use the mail. The procedure usually is to answer an advertisement and use a cover address as the return address. If the con involves falsely advertised merchandise which is never delivered, the sales literature and the canceled check serve as evidence. In other types of fraud, such as the variants on the "prisoner" theme, the correspondence from the suspect is carefully filed for later use in prosecution. In some instances, there may be a justification for a mail cover. The requirement is that the mail cover will lead to locating a fugitive or developing information about a felony or attempted felony.

A major problem with fraudulent mail offers is that the operators are fairly sophisticated. They understand that postal inspectors have to move rather slowly in their investigations, and often don't become aware of a mail fraud until a defrauded customer complains. The sharp operator will, therefore, place his ads and collect the money for a few weeks, and abandon the operation before the postal inspectors can mobilize. By the time an investigation begins, the operator has abandoned the address and left town. By using an assumed name for his scam, he can make tracing him almost impossible.

Many types of criminal cases lead to overlapping jurisdictions between the postal inspectors and local police.[3] In many instances there is close cooperation between the two agencies. One cooperative case involved interstate coupon fraud by retailers.

Postal inspectors became aware that some retailers were turning in coupons that they themselves had clipped from newspapers or gotten in the mail. Manufacturers found it difficult to prove that the coupons had not been legitimately collected. Postal inspectors had coupons printed for fictitious products, and mailed them to retailers. In New York, postal inspectors placed ads for "Breen" detergent in newspapers, complete with coupons. Retailers who redeemed them for cash found themselves being prosecuted. Members of a Texas coupon-counterfeiting ring found themselves charged with mail fraud.[4]

Some large-scale embezzlers use post office boxes or mail drops to support dummy companies that play major roles in their scams. One executive defrauded his employer, GTE Spacenet, out of $249,000 by creating false invoices and having payments sent to mailing addresses of fictitious companies. The scheme came to light when diligent auditors discovered that no such companies existed.[5]

In the case of drug enforcement, police have ready access to printed material. At least one police force (Howard County, Maryland) subscribes to the magazine *High Times* for "intelligence purposes."[6] A spokesman for the police agency, Corporal Randolph W. Roby, admits only to monitoring the "street price of drugs in different areas." There are other aspects to drug enforcement, however.

Some small businessmen make a living from selling the raw materials and laboratory equipment for manufacturing illegal drugs. It's a quirk of the law that, although the drugs themselves are outlawed, the materials and equipment for making them are not.

The Drug Enforcement Administration, attempting to infiltrate those who are or who might be producing such drugs, places ads in various publications advertising such materials to build up a suspect list. This operation was similar to "Operation Looking Glass," above. The DEA used the names of "fronts," cover companies, located around the country. Some of these are: "Apex Publishing Company," New York; "Buckeye Scientific Company," Columbus, Ohio; "North Central Industrial Chemicals," Elk Grove Village, Illinois; "Precision Chemical Company," "Universal Solvents of America," Westmont, Illinois; and "Vara Scientific," Newark, New Jersey. They advertise in publications which they feel may attract a "drug culture" readership, such as *High Times*, and *Biker Lifestyle*. The ads don't mention the chemicals, but advertise catalogs in which these items are listed. Respondents wind up on a "target list."[7]

Penetration of Mail Drops

One aspect of police undercover work is the deep secrecy in which police agencies conduct it. This is both logical and normal, as undercover operators who are "blown" can lose their lives in some situations. The other side of the coin is that there is great potential for abuses because of this secrecy. As it stands, there's no court order needed for an undercover operation as there is for a police search or a wiretap.

Police investigators have always had a tendency to go on "fishing expeditions," conducting investigations even where there's no clear evidence of a crime. Some have dignified the practice with the term "proactive policing," but it's still "fishing." One way to fish in the mail drop field is to have a police undercover agent apply for employment at a mail drop to scrutinize the operation for criminal activity.

Once in place, the agent will keep his or her eyes and ears open for anything useful. Without a specific crime to investigate, this is simply fishing, or meddling, but an enthusiastic undercover agent can find something to justify the investigation. This is akin to the practice of finding another charge, such as "resisting arrest" or "assaulting an officer" to cover police officers who make a false arrest. Particularly dishonest agents will simply "plant" evidence, such as drugs. Others will act as *agent provocateurs* or arrange to observe a contrived "crime," such as discarding mail. In some instances, envelopes for people unknown at the mail drop will be delivered. Any operator who discards such mail instead of returning it to the post office risks prosecution.

Law enforcement exploitation of mail drops for various purposes will continue unabated. The main reason is because its primary use is to gather "leads," which never wind up in court. This enables law officers to operate in total secrecy on their fishing expeditions, and this secrecy allows them total latitude.

Notes:

1. Scripps Howard News Service, April 6, 1986.

2. Miles, John G., Richardson, David B., and Scudellari, Anthony E., *The Law Officer's Pocket Manual*, Washington, DC, Bureau of National Affairs, 1995, p. 7:35.
3. *Training Key, Volume Ten*, International Association of Chiefs of Police, pp. 13-18.
4. "Coupon Criminals, Please Cut it Out," *U.S. News & World Report*, February 12, 1990, p. 19.
5. "Former GTE Spacenet Official Charged With Mail Fraud," *Data Channels*, January 24, 1990, p. 7.
6. Kaysing, Bill, *Privacy: How to Get it. How to Enjoy it*, Fountain Valley, CA, 1977, p. 3.
7. Interview with Michael Kuzma, former manager of the now-defunct M.K. & Associates, a remail service.

Introduction to Part II

Now that you've got a good introduction to the field of secret addresses and the other choices, it's time to examine the ramifications for you. You'll find in this section some vital information regarding how to find a mail drop, and how to monitor it to make sure that the operator is serving you well. You'll also find some tips on how to work on a shoestring, including one method of creating a false address that costs you nothing at all.

You'll learn how to make use of a mail drop if you want to vanish and avoid betraying yourself. You'll gain an insight into how anyone trying to trace your might go about it.

At times, you may have reason to suspect that a person with whom you're dealing by mail is not all he claims to be. If you're geographically close, you can inspect the premises yourself to be sure that the party is genuine. Otherwise, you'll have to use some direct and indirect techniques which we'll review together.

Chapter Eleven:
Seeking Services:
What's Right For You?

When you decide to get a private mailing address, you'll have to consider exactly what you need and balance this against cost and convenience. You'll have to decide whether the extra services available for a fee are really worth the money. You'll have to consider postal boxes versus mail drops against secretarial services.

You'll probably also want to consider the other choices available. One way is to have a friend or relative receive mail for you. The limitation on this is that the volume can't be too much or it can strain the relationship. Over time, he may get tired of forwarding your mail and not be as prompt as you would like. If you're expecting checks, this can really hurt you. Another aspect is the prospect of unwelcome visitors showing up in front of his door.

General delivery is a way for you to pick up your mail directly from the post office without the charge that goes with a postal box. You don't need a street address. There are two problems with general delivery, though. The first is that you must pick up your mail at a postal window during normal business hours. You also have to show I.D. Another problem is that the post office will only hold your mail ten days or two weeks before returning it to the sender.

Another way of setting up a secret address is to rent a room in a rooming house for a residential address, or a one-room office if you need a business address in a business location. This will cost much more than any other choice, especially as rents can be quite high in some locales. There are some compensating factors, though.

One is that the transaction, when dealing with a residential renter, can be in cash without raising any suspicions. Another is that the secret address does not require that any form be filed with the post office or landlord. You simply come to pick up your mail at convenient times, and that's that. An extra fee, accompanied by a good cover story, can even persuade the landlord or his agent to forward your mail if you request. You may tell the landlord that you're a traveling businessman and that you spend most of your time on the road. This will quell any suspicions that might arise when the landlord notices that you're usually not home.

Renting in a business locale requires a different approach in order to avoid problems and suspicions. If you show up in a "power suit" with an expensive briefcase, you'll proclaim yourself as legitimate, and quiet suspicions. You can be certain that the rental agent won't ask you for I.D., even when you give him a check. Naturally, you'll have a company checkbook in the briefcase. The renter has no worry that you'll pick up the building and walk away with it. The agent may or may not become aware that you're simply using the premises as a mailing address. You can forestall his curiosity by telling him at the outset that your business causes you to travel a lot, which will explain your long absences.

With a large enough budget, you can even hire a receptionist to staff the office. She can forward the mail and answer the phone, taking messages which you can obtain when you check in. This will enhance the usefulness of the rental. It can even be a "branch office" of your company, real or imaginary. The ease of long-distance direct dialing means that you can return calls from another area of the country without the other party becoming aware that you're not on the premises.

Resource Finders

There are several ways to find what you need. The first and easiest is looking in the Yellow Pages. Mail drops may be listed under "Mail Receiving Services" or similar classifications. The listings under "Secretarial Services" contain business operators offering more extensive and higher-class services.

The Yellow Pages provide local listings. For mail drops outside your area, you might find out-of-state telephone directories at the local library, but these might not cover the area of interest to you. Official telephone company directories are the most accurate listings. There are, however, other choices that offer more convenience, but less accuracy, for out-of-area listings.

Computerized telephone directories, covering the entire country, are available at most computer software outlets. Two major brands are Selectphone and Phone Directory. Computerized directories vary greatly in quality, and most claim to be the most accurate in the field. The highest accuracy figure claimed is 84 percent, and even this is questionable.

The reason is that, unlike the telephone companies' databases, which are used for official telephone company directories and available to directory assistance operators, CD-ROM directories are only updated annually. Americans are very mobile, and changes of address and phone numbers are late in arriving onto CD-ROMs, whereas the telephone companies records changes daily.

Another problem is that CD-ROM phone directory producers update only one quarter of their databases at a time, selling "new" editions every three months. In fact, you receive a totally updated database only once a year, a gimmick the manufacturers aren't eager to explain to potential buyers.

This drawback isn't as serious as it might seem when you're searching for a mail drop. Individuals tend to relocate more often than businesses, and when you're seeking a mail drop an outdated listing can even be an asset. A mail drop that has recently moved isn't the best bet, because you need a stable business, not one that might be gone tomorrow.

Some cheapie CD-ROM directories are programmed to allow only 5,000 retrievals before locking up, forcing the customer to buy another program. It's possible to defeat this feature, though. The way to do it is to understand that the program puts a dated file in the hard drive's root directory. This prevents reinstalling when the 5,000 limit is used up. After you install the program, scan the root directory for a file bearing that date and time, using the search feature of your DOS program. Make a note of the file's name and date. When you reach the 5,000 limit, go into your root directory again and delete that file. Then reinstall the program.

A trade association that provides referrals for its over 525 members in the United States is:

Associated Mail and Parcel Centers
705 School Street
Napa, CA 94559
Telephone: (800) 365-2672
Attn: Charmaine Fennie, Executive Director

If you're interested in obtaining an offshore mail drop, a mail drop service based in Liechtenstein provides both a Swiss address and two in Balzers, Liechtenstein:

Treu Comm AG
Heiligweis 23, Postfach 159
9496 Balzers, Liechtenstein
Phone: 075/388 00 20
Fax: 075/388 00 40

Treu Comm AG
Postfach 1228
FL-9490 Vaduz, Liechtenstein

The Swiss address is:

Treu Comm AG
Postfach 48
FL-9477 Trubbach, Switzerland

Treu Comm AG provides several services of interest to businesses, including mail receiving and forwarding, mailings from either address, secretarial services, telephone message service, and meeting rooms. Other services are available on an individually negotiated basis.

Treu Comm AG emphasizes that discretion is part of the service. While the boxholder must disclose his true address to Treu Comm AG, the company will give it out only by instruction from the customer. Treu Comm AG's brochure also states that: "The services will be discontinued if the charges and fees are not paid on time and if illegal, dubious, or credibility damaging business dealings or actions are carried out."

Making Choices

If you're on a very tight budget, a post office box will be the best way to go. Despite the well-documented inefficiency of the U.S. Postal Service, a P.O. box can be the cheapest buy. The price of a postal box varies with size, the locale, and the demand. Postal boxes in large cities are more expensive than those in rural post offices, as a rule. Rental period is six months. A typical rate is $20 for the smallest box, escalating to $29, $52, and $84 for the largest.

Private operators are not necessarily competitive. There are usually two price scales, personal and business. One price list offered at the time of writing (early 1996) charged $10 per three months for the smallest-size personal box, $14 for the intermediate size, and $18 for the largest.

The difference between personal and business mail drop boxes is that business boxes allow listing the business name and two personal names. Three-month charges for business boxes are $14 for the smallest, $18 for the intermediate size, and $24 for the largest. A $5 key deposit is required on all rentals.

Discounts are available, but only from private mail drops. The mail drop surveyed offered an extra month free with a six-month rental and three free months with a one-year rental.

The big drawback of a post office box is that the address always reads like a post office box. Another drawback, which can stop you cold, is that often there are no boxes available in your locale. This is an important reason why private mail drop operators prosper. A collateral effect of a waiting list for post office boxes is that their prices will be about the same as those that private mail drops charge, an effect of supply and demand.

If you've decided to hire a mail drop, the first thing to look for is one with a street address. Don't bother with any mail drops that work out of a P.O. box unless your purpose is just to "get lost," in which case the address is unimportant. Keep in mind the district in which the address is, and its suitability for your purpose. If you're trying to foster the illusion of a residential address, one in the business district will seem odd to anyone who knows the area. If your correspondents are from other parts of the country, this is less of a problem.

If you're using the mail drop to obtain false I.D., you have to be aware that a clerk in the drivers license bureau might wonder about a business district address listed on a drivers license application as a "residence." Another point is that, if you're trying to obtain credit cards, banks will expect a street address, not a post office box. If you're also job-hunting, employers expect the applicant to provide a street address. The exception is if you're new in town and explain to prospective employers that you haven't yet established residence.

If you're claiming that your address is residential, and you engage a service that operates out of a post office box, you're paying a premium price and losing half the value at the outset because any of your correspondents seeing that address will know right off that it's not a street address. To maintain the illusion of a legitimate street address, ask whether or not the mail drop operator requires that the mailing address be coded with a "suite" number or box number. Some operators sort their mail by box number, not by name, and including a box number in an address can also be a giveaway. In that connection, make sure that the operator's mailing address does not include a suite number in itself if you're trying to present the illusion that the address is residential. A mail drop in a large office building may have a suite number as well as a box number.

There are several ways of masking the box number if you have no choice. One is to list it on the address as an "apartment" number. Another is to write it as a "department" number, which works only if you're running a business. If the mail drop is in a suite, you can include the box number after a hyphen. The address will then look like this:

ABC Company, Suite 1234-56
123 45th Street
Anytown, USA, 00000

If secrecy is your main concern, you'd better give a lot of thought to how much of a risk you're taking with the operator. Many, as a matter of integrity, won't give out the identity of a box holder unless faced with a court order or subpoena. Others can be bribed cheaply.

The safest way to avoid problems is to not give your true identity or address. Fill out the Form 1583 with a totally false name and address. You may have to support this with false I.D. Remember that one copy stays on file with the operator and one goes to the post office, which does not check it out. Regulation 153.211 of the *Domestic Mail Manual* requires the operator to ask for two items of identification, and list them on the form. It also states that postal authorities will not check out the I.D. unless the postal inspector suspects that some criminal activity might be involved .

Some operators are careless about checking I.D. and don't bother. If the operator asks for I.D., simply pat your pocket and announce that you forgot your checkbook. Tell him that you're going home for it and get out quickly. If there's no I.D. required, just pay cash.

One way to avoid giving an address is possible in a seaport. Telling the box operator that you're a seaman and live on a ship may get you by. He may ask for a seaman's card though, in which case you simply tell him that you left it aboard ship. Another way is to state that you're a tourist with no fixed address. You might, if you're female, claim that you don't even have a drivers license because your husband does all of the driving.

However, be aware that today many mail drop operators ask for a drivers license and will make a photocopy of it to keep on file. Most states have drivers licenses that are hard to forge because of a state seal on the photograph or a reflective pattern on the surface. A Polaroid photo just won't do if you have to take your forged license out of your wallet so that the mail drop operator can make a photocopy. In this case, another person's license if the photograph resembles you, will do. Lost or stolen I.D is often available in metropolitan areas.

A good factor to consider if you're worried that a determined tracer might want to "stake out" the mail drop is whether the operator offers lobby keys for the convenience of those who want to pick up their mail at odd hours. Not all do. This allows you the choice of picking up your mail during the very early morning hours, when nobody else is likely to be around, and, when you can easily note anyone staking out the mail drop. Also, pick up your mail only once a week, and never twice on the same day. This makes it necessary for anyone trying to trace you to invest a lot of surveillance time. Private investigators tend to be both lazy and venal, often trying to avoid real work. For the same reason, never call ahead to find out if you have mail. If the operator's in collusion with the tracer, it lets him know when you're coming.

One good way of making counter-surveillance easier is to select a mail drop located in a shopping center. This allows you to drive by and check the parking lot for watchers. It also makes it more difficult for a watcher to get close enough to see which box a client is opening. This isn't absolute protection, but it helps.

Application for Delivery of Mail Through Agent

	1. Date

In consideration of delivery of my or our mail to the agent named below, the addressee and agent agree that: (1) the Postal Service will not forward my or our mail on a change of address order upon termination of this agency relationship; (2) the forwarding or return of my or our mail is the responsibility of the agent; (3) all mail, including letters and other First Class mail, delivered to the agent under this authorization must be prepaid with new postage when redeposited in the mails; (4) that upon request, the agent will provide to the Postal Service, all addresses to which the agent forwards mail.

NOTE: The applicant must execute this form in duplicate in the presence of the agent, his authorized employee, or a notary public. The agent retains a signed copy in such manner that it is available for examination by postal representatives.

This application may be subject to verification procedures by the U S Postal Service to substantiate that the applicant resides or conducts business at the home or business address listed in boxes 4b or 5a.

TO: Postmaster

2. Name(s) in which applicant's mail will be received for delivery to agent	3. Applicant authorizes delivery to and in care of (Name, address and ZIP code of agent)
4. Name of applicant	4a. Identification Two (2) types identification required. Agent must write in identifying information 1.
4b. Home address (Number, street, city, state and ZIP code) Telephone number	2.
5. Name of firm or corporation	Acceptable identification include: Drivers License, Military or other Government ID, Passport, National Credit Cards, Alien Registration Card and Birth Certificate
5a. Business address (Name, street and ZIP code) Telephone number	6. Kind of Business
7. If applicant is a firm: name each member whose mail is to be delivered	8. If a CORPORATION, give names and addresses of its officers

9. If business name of the address (Corporation or Trade Name) has been registered, give name of county and state, and date of registration

10. References (Name, address and ZIP code)	Warning: The furnishing of false information on this form may result in a fine of not more than $10,000 or imprisonment of not more than 5 years, or both (18 U S C 1001)
Signature of agent Notary Public	Signature of applicant (If firm or corporation, application must be signed by officer. Show title.)

PRIVACY ACT: The collection of this information is authorized by 39 USC 403, 404. It serves as the written authority for the delivery of mail other than as addressed. As a routine use, this information may be disclosed to an appropriate law enforcement agency for investigative or prosecution proceedings, to a congressional office at your request, to a labor organization as required by the NLRA, and where pertinent in a legal proceeding to which the Postal Service is a party. Completion of this form is voluntary, however if this information is not provided the mail will be withheld from delivery to the agent and delivered to the addressee, or if the address of the addressee is that of the agent, returned to the sender.

PS Form 1583, October 1990   *U.S. Government Printing Office: 1991 — 282-404/44833

Postal Service Form 1583: Application for Delivery of Mail Through Agent.

Another precaution is to be wary of strange packages that you did not expect. Unordered merchandise wrapped in bright paper is a technique which is used to ease the task of anyone staking out the box. Another is a distinctively shaped package, such as a four-foot long mailing tube. There's more information on this technique in the discussion on methods used for tracing.

If you trust the integrity of the mail drop operator, you can have him forward your mail to your home. This avoids the need for you to visit his premises, as you can send him a check or money order for the rental and other fees. If you need to preserve total anonymity, payment can be by money order, as a bank or post office does not require I.D. to sell a money order.

Problems With Mail Drops

Hiring a mail drop doesn't solve all problems. Junk mail, for example, will follow you. If you have a mail box at your curb, or an apartment mail box, you'll often find your first-class letters creased and even torn because the mail carrier crammed everything into the box. Magazines to which you subscribe end up with covers torn as the post office drone stuffs catalogs into the box alongside them.

The problem has gotten worse in recent years, partly because the post office allows cheap bulk rates to junk mailers, and they take advantage of this. Third-class mail, for example, comprised 31 percent of all mail in 1981. By 1989, the proportion had risen to 39 percent.[1]

Fund-raising is a growth industry in this country, and you can expect a deluge of cleverly worded appeals which are designed to pry dollars from you.[2] Fund-raising letters have proliferated, not because they're so effective, but because they contribute to the livelihood of fund-raising organizations. As much as 90 percent of the money raised by non-profit groups merely goes for more mailing to raise more money, and to keep junk mailers gainfully employed.[3]

The problem with fund-raising letters is that you can never satisfy them. Once you send a contribution, your name goes on a special list and you'll receive even more appeals. Fund-raisers also sell their sucker lists to other fund-raisers, because the names of people who have proven susceptible to mailed fund-raising letters are of immense value to others seeking to tap their generosity or gullibility.

Likewise, unsolicited catalogs and other debris. Aggravating this is that the post office sells lists of those who have filed change of address cards to junk mailers.[4] However, a private mail drop can relieve you of some of the aggravation of the barrage of junk mail.

First, the post office simply will not forward most junk mail which is sent at bulk rates. Another benefit is that a competent and conscientious mail drop operator can simply stack excess mail in a convenient spot, instead of trying to cram it all into your mail box as do the post office drones.

However, mailing list compilers are very aggressive, and you can't escape junk mail completely, as some catalogs will arrive addressed merely to "Occupant." Other junk mailers obtain your name from lists of credit card holders, subscription lists, and other sources that junk mail list compilers sell on computer discs.

One way of gaining satisfaction is to retaliate against junk mailers by making them lose money on you. Open each envelope to check for a prepaid business reply envelope or card. Write in a totally fictitious name and address, and drop it in the mail. The junk mailer will have to pay return postage, and he'll waste resources sending the goods or subscription to a non-existent person. While fighting your pin-prick war against junk mailers, you may doubt its effectiveness, but remember that the profit margin in junk mail is very slim, and only a few losses can be very painful for the junk mailer.

A private mail box also cannot spare you the problems of post office inefficiency. Despite "guaranteeing" next-day delivery for overnight express packets, the post office often is late, and there's nothing you can do about shoddy post office performance.[5] You can, however, choose an alternative. What you can do is use a private service, such as UPS or Federal Express, which really does deliver when promised. Remember, a private mail drop will accept parcels from UPS and FedEx, while the post office won't.

It's also important to discriminate between a genuine private mail-receiving business and a post office subcontractor. Some business owners operate mail drops or postal contract stations to bring in more potential customers, calling this "traffic-building."[6] A post office contract station is not a mail drop, although it may resemble one, and will not offer the many services a private mail drop can.

There are also problems with certain mail drops. Some mail drop operators are simply "flakes" and are not very reliable, even about putting the mail in the proper boxes. This is why it's important to select one that's either recommended by friends or one that's been operating in the same location for several years.

Eyeball a mail drop before you even ask about the rates. Look at the location as a start. Is the location in the sort of area you want? Is there adequate parking, or do you have to compete with the crush of traffic going into the liquor store next door? As you stroll by, note if there is a line inside the mail drop. Some mail drops are so busy that they can't hire enough people to take care of the traffic, and there will be a delay in putting mail into the boxes.

The mail drop business is a volatile one, and small operators come and go. If one closes its doors, you may never get your mail. You'll also have to alert all of your correspondents to your new address, which can be a nuisance.

A franchised operator is more likely to be stable. Mail Boxes, Etc. is one nationwide franchise that has a good track record. The franchise operator who has invested his savings is motivated to make his business run smoothly.[7] However, don't take for granted that every franchisee is competent and stable. Check it out yourself.

One way to check the stability of a mail drop is to look up previous issues of the Yellow Pages. Some libraries keep old ones on file for several years. A better and simpler way is to photocopy the mail drop listings in your Yellow Pages now if you don't need a mail drop today. This is a precaution against the possibility of your needing one next year, or even later, and will give you a good list of the ones which have been in business in the same locations for several years.

Even when things are going well, it's prudent to check up on the operation once in a while. Sending yourself an envelope to see if you receive it within a reasonable time is a good way. Another way to check the integrity or competence of an operator is to have one or more of your correspondents number their envelopes or letters.[8] This will alert you to any missing from the sequence.

One drawback to a private mail drop arises when you change your address. If you're operating a business, this can be a serious problem. You cannot file a postal change of address card in this case, because the post office will not sort the mail addressed to a private mail-receiving service to pick out mail addressed to you, which means you'll have to notify all of your correspondents individually of your new address.

This makes it squarely your task to get your mail forwarded, one way or another. Note that a private mail service charges for forwarding your mail. The operator stuffs your mail into a large envelope and sends it to your new address. There will certainly be a charge for postage, and he may tack on a handling charge.

Mail drop operators know this, and some take advantage of the great inconvenience you suffer by providing sloppy service, such as delaying sorting out the mail after they receive it. They know you're at their mercy. One mail drop operator responded to a business customer's complaint about poor service by threatening to cut off his mail delivery. This is a very important reason to make sure of the service before you sign up and begin receiving mail there.

If worse comes to worst, and service deteriorates to the point where it's intolerable, the best way to deal with it is to get out without raising a fuss. Don't let your ire show because the operator can hurt you by delaying or "losing" your mail. Begin by hiring another mail drop, and notify your contacts of the new address. When all of your mail is coming to the new service, simply don't renew the old one.

If your need for revenge is important, you can retaliate by filling out magazine subscription cards in the old operator's name and address. This is effective because it hits him right where he lives, choking his mailbag with unwanted mail, and impeding him in the conduct of his business because he has to sort it out himself.

Security First

If security is your main concern, you have to be prepared to pay a price. For example, if you're running away from the "mob," you have a good incentive to take all possible precautions. The basic one is to use only mail drops that also offer mail forwarding.

This is because one way of assuring security is to use a chain of drops, instructing each operator to forward your mail to the next one. This is because you have to face the risk that some mail drop operators will sell out their clients. If you have only one secret address, and the operator sells you out, that's the ball game. Arranging a chain of drops, with one forwarding your mail to the next one, makes it much more difficult for a tracer. To trace you successfully, all operators must disclose the address where they send your mail.

To break the trail even more, you might have one or more mail drops in a foreign country. This is especially valuable for evading a police investigation. The tradition of cooperation between police agencies breaks down when crossing national barriers. We've seen an excellent example of this in the way that the police of Latin American countries have withheld wholehearted cooperation from American cops when drugs are the issue.

Part of the price you pay is time. Each transaction will take several days, and you may find your mail seriously delayed. Another part of the price is the money you'll spend for fees and postage. It's customary to establish an account with a mail forwarder. To minimize the frequency of contacts it's best to pay at least one hundred dollars into the account at the outset, as this has to cover mailbox rental, forwarding charges, if any, and certainly postage for forwarding your mail .

Tip! To minimize the fees, choose mail drops in areas that don't have long waiting lists for post office boxes. If postal boxes are scarce, mail drop operators, as well as postmasters, jack up their prices accordingly.

All told, you can get a lot of use from a mail drop if you choose carefully, take nothing for granted, and practice security. A little paranoia goes a long way. Keep in mind that paranoids get victimized too.

Notes:

1. "Junk Mail is Bulking Up," *USA Today*, October 11, 1990, p. 1D.
2. Kinsley, Michael, "The Check is in The Mail," *Time*, April 9, 1990, p 98.
3. Smolowe, Jill, "READ THIS!!!!!!," *Time*, November 26, 1990, p. 62.
4. Cauchon, Dennis, "Post Office Helps Junk Follow You," *USA Today*, May 14, 1992, p. 1A.
5. Davis, Fred, "The Postal Service Couldn't Be Worse," *USA Today*, November 13, 1990, p. 10A.
6. "Mailing Centers Becoming Latest Traffic-building Strategy," *Drug Store News*, February 19, 1990, p. 52.
7. Garrett, Echo Montgomery, "Mailbox Missionary; Anthony DeSio Takes on the Post Office," *Success*, March, 1990, v37, p. 62.
8. Peterson, Kay, *Survival of the Snowbirds*, Estes Park, CO, Roving Press Publications, 1982, p. 156.

Chapter Twelve:
A Quick And Cheap Fake Address

A simple and quick way to establish a fake address is to use a post office change of address and mail forwarding form. This form, #3575, is available without charge at any post office.

Here's how you use it: Decide upon your purpose. If you're using the fake address to give you an "image," for example a mirage address in a high-rent business district, you select the address of a large and high-class office building. On the other hand, if you want to appear to live in a prestigious neighborhood, choose the address of a luxury apartment house. You list that address as the old one, and list your real address, post office box, or mail drop as the forwarding address. The post office will forward any mail addressed to you at the old address to the forwarding address you list. You need never to have actually lived or worked there.

One reason why this works is the general incompetence, high turnover, and demoralization among postal employees. While many seek to hold on to their government jobs, the frequent change of assignments and routes means that they rarely get to know all of the tenants on their routes. They'll accept a mail forwarding notice without undue curiosity.

The great advantage of this technique is that you never have to come into contact with any postal employee. You simply pick up a form, fill it out, and drop it into any mail box. The drawback is that anyone who knows about common mail-tracing methods can find your true address, or at least the one to which the mail goes from the change order. This means that your security is limited, and that the main value of this quick technique is to obtain a high-prestige address without paying the fee for a box.

Is this illegal? Maybe. Form 3575 contains a threatening notice stating that "Anyone submitting a false or inaccurate statement on this card is subject to punishment by fine or imprisonment or both under Section 2, 1001, 1702, and 1708 of Title 18 of the United States Code." Anyone who looks up those sections of Title 18 will find out that they have to do with obstructing, stealing, or diverting the mail, not creating a false address. The irony of this is that it's definitely illegal to divert someone's mail as a harassing technique, yet it's almost impossible to find the person who did it. Finding the addressee of a false address and forwarding order is simple, but prosecution is another matter since he's only redirecting his own mail.

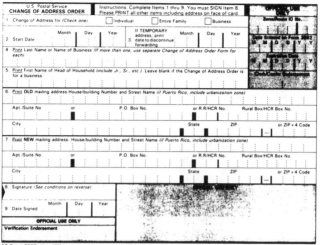

PS Form 3575, June 1993

Both sides of Postal Service Form 3575: Change of Address Order.

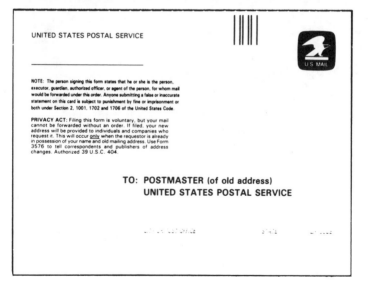

Chapter Thirteen:
Using Mail Drops To Vanish

Anyone planning to disappear for whatever reason may find a mail drop worth having. The reason is that some people like to maintain certain correspondence and certain relationships by mail. Magazine subscriptions, for example, are important to some people, but they also serve as a way to trace an individual if he sends a change of address order to the publisher.[1]

Changing Identities

"Disappearing" often includes a change of identity to make it more difficult to trace you through your Social Security number, union affiliation, etc. A mail drop is one way of putting distance between yourself and your former life.[2]

Another identifier which can betray you is your Social Security number. If you apply for employment, you'll find this laying a paper trail right to you. You can give your employer a false one, and work on that particular job for many months before the investigation gathers momentum, but if you plan to make it a long-term affair you'll need a new Social Security number. A mail drop helps in the quest for new I.D., as long as it's not a post office box.[3] Let's see why:

Using a post office box is a less costly method of receiving mail, but it can be a "lead" to you. A moderately secure way of using a post office box is to obtain it legally before you have to vanish. Once you move, continue to use the box but don't notify them of your move. You can continue to pick up mail at your box without anyone tracing you if the effort to find you is not too serious. Also be aware that if there's any problem with your paperwork, there might be a postal inspector waiting when you come to claim your mail.

Obtaining a new drivers license requires a mail drop if you don't want to use your new address.[4] It's more discreet to use a mail drop because it breaks the trail and makes quick-and-easy tracing impossible. An important point to watch is getting a mail drop address that doesn't scream "mail drop" because of a box number, and to get one in a residential neighborhood.

Keeping the Secret

Let's look at the other side of the hill for a moment to see what's involved in tracing you through a post office box. First, the person seeking you out has to know that you have a P.O. box. If you're running away from your wife, she will know if you've told her. If you haven't, your secret is probably safe. Truly, nobody needs to know that you have post office box unless you choose to tell them .

Nobody "needs to know," but some people may get to know that you have post office box. What do you do with your magazines? Do you leave them lying around with their mailing labels? That is a sure tip-off to anyone who uses his eyes and his common sense.

If you've let the secret slip, anyone seeking you still has the problem of finding you. The only way for a private individual trace you through a post office box is to put a 24-hour watch on the box and shadow the person who picks up the mail. This is expensive in manpower, and you can minimize the danger by picking up your mail only once a week. Police agencies can, of course, obtain the identity of a post office box renter with minimal fuss.

Getting magazines at a mail drop is somewhat more secure if you have the operator forward it. The point is to forward it to another mail drop where you pick it up. If you want to be supercautious, hire yet another mail drop to insert yet another cut-out. This will delay your mail even more, and you must balance the loss of convenience against the risk. Counting all the costs and delays involved, it's better and safer to buy your magazines off the rack.

Establishing an Employment History

One aspect of vanishing is supporting yourself. Unless you've departed with a lot of money, you'll need to find employment. Almost every employer will want to know about your previous work experience. The application requires information on previous employment.

Small employers tend not to check up on claimed experience or references listed in the application, especially if the job is in a skilled trade. Either you "work out" in his shop or you don't, and previous employment has little to do with that immediate question. If you look good, sound good, and show that you can do the work, your employer won't be very curious about additional details.

Larger companies have personnel departments, and they're staffed by people who are paid to run "background checks." To cope with this, you need at least a mail drop, and possibly a telephone-answering service to set up a dummy former employer. In some cases, a personnel department staffer will actually write or phone the companies or references you list.[5] In this case, you should be prepared to answer with a reply on the alleged company's letterhead.

If you're using a new name, or if you don't want to be found, it's bad tactics to list actual former employers. They might be a way for a tracer to find you, and would be an impediment because they only know you by your former name.

One point that's important to make at the outset is that you can go only so far with setting up mail drops and covers to support a faked employment history. If anyone checks even halfway, you'll need more than one mail drop. There are two ways of discouraging or deterring intensive inquiries:

1. Don't list any phone numbers for your alleged former employers .
2. List only out-of-town firms.

You can always enlist a friend to support your story, giving his address as that of a former employee on the application form. If you want to take the risk, you can even list his telephone number, but he would then be obligated to answer his phone with the name of the supposed company or the last four digits of his number, to avoid giving you away if anyone actually calls. He would also have to be there during business hours, and this could be difficult if he holds a job.

Modern technology has provided an answer, however. If your accomplice has a cellular telephone, you can list that number. The cellular phone presumably goes with your friend wherever he goes, and a personnel department employee calling long-distance would have no way of knowing that this particular local exchange is reserved for cellular phones.

It's important to be realistic about one point: Certain fields will be closed to you because the background check is too intensive. If you apply for any sort of government job, especially with the Defense Department or the police, you'll find that investigators will do a "positive vetting" job on you. "Positive vetting" means that they are not content with simply a negative investigation. That your name does not turn up on any "wanted" list isn't enough. They're seeking positive evidence that you are whom you say you are. They will also check to see that you were born where you say you were, went to school where you say you did, and look into the details of your alleged employment history and even personal life. They'll visit your former employers and alleged neighbors.

The investigation will be even more thorough if you apply for a job which requires a security clearance from the Department of Defense. The "secret" clearance questionnaire is eight pages long, and each detail you list will be checked out. Applications for "top secret" and higher clearances are even longer and more detailed.

This depth of investigation will quickly break through any mail drop cover you've built up for yourself. You might find it hard to believe, but government investigators have the time and manpower to check out every detail listed and even some not listed. For example, the Defense Industrial Security Clearance Office (DISCO) has offices in every major city in the country, and claiming that you are from another state won't impede the investigation at all, because there will be agents nearby to check out your story. If, for example, you claim to have attended a certain college, an agent will check out the records in the college office to verify this. He'll also interview your former professors to verify that they remember you. If necessary, agents will trace former classmates to check what they have to say about you. They'll also go to the address you listed while attending school to verify that you actually lived there, and to solicit the landlord's and neighbors' opinions of you.

DISCO investigators make house calls. They won't stop at verifying employment history by phone, but will visit your supposed former employers to interview them. They'll also personally check out the addresses where you stated you had lived at that time.

It's simply too much effort to build up an unbreakable cover for certain jobs. It may even be impossible, if the investigation is more than casual and superficial. This is why basic strategy dictates that you stick to jobs which won't attract that much attention.

Don't Start a New Trail to Yourself

Equally important as getting away is avoiding creating new traces that can lead to you. At times, you may have a need to mail something into your old world. This may be a letter to a friend or relative, or it may be paying off a debt.

It doesn't matter how trustworthy the addressee may be. His silence may be as deep as the grave, but this won't prevent someone seeing the return address or the postmark on your envelope. Of course, you aren't that dumb: you would not put a return address on the envelope. The postmark can give you away, though, especially if you're now living in a small town. This is the time to use a remailing service.[6]

A remailer will accept mail from you and post them from his location. Some offer remailing from overseas locales, an especially good way to lose your trail and frustrate anyone trying to trace you.[7]

You find a remailing service the same way you find mail drops. However, the only ones useful to you are those away from your area, which is why the local Yellow Pages won't be helpful. Finding the Yellow Pages from other cities in the local library will be more fruitful. So will looking in the mail drop directories. Yet another way is looking in the classified sections of magazines which carry mail drop ads, such as the mechanical magazines and the sexually oriented ones.

The best way, of course, is to prepare in advance. Selecting remailers before making the escape is the simplest and best, because it also allows time to send test letters to determine if the remailer is actually doing his job. Having several remail envelopes full of blank paper is better than entrusting a valuable piece of mail to one on a first-time basis.

It's still possible to vanish in this country, despite the tremendous array of investigative techniques available today. With the proper preparation, and enough money to finance your move until you can find employment, you can appear to have dropped into a black hole.

Notes:

1. *100 Ways To Disappear and Live Free*, Fountain Valley, CA, Eden Press, 1985, p. 5.
2. Anonymous, *New I.D. In America*, Boulder, CO, Paladin Press, 1983, pp. 50-53.
3. Clark, Gary B., *How To Get Lost and Start All Over Again*, Port Townsend, WA, Loompanics Unlimited, 1986, p. 70.
4. *Ibid.*, pp. 35-36.
5. *Ibid.*, pp. 72-78.

6. Richmond, Doug, *How Disappear Completely and Never Be Found,* Port Townsend, WA, Loompanics Unlimited, 1986, pp. 100-101.
7. Budd, Wayne, *The Official Remailing Guide, Eighth Edition*, Eldorado, Ontario, Canada, 1993, pp. 15-16.

Chapter Fourteen: How To Tell If Your Correspondent Is Using A Mail Drop

In certain instances it's useful to know if the person with whom you're dealing is using his real address or a mail drop. A mail drop can be a sign that something is amiss. While a number of legitimate businesses, especially those engaged in mail-order, use post office boxes for extra security, they're open about it. The customer can understand the need for limiting access to envelopes that contain money orders, checks, and sometimes cash.

Some fly-by-night operators advertise merchandise, collect the orders and the money that goes with them, and disappear. A measure of protection is always to order as late as possible, in the hope that the crooked operators have already gone by the time your check gets there. It's better yet never to order anything when the seller tries to impose a time limit. If it's legitimate, he'll be selling it again next month or next year.

Another precaution is to check for a mail drop. There are some warning signs:

♦ Any address that includes a box number, however disguised, might be a mail drop. Sometimes it's listed as

"Suite #." If it's a business, the suite number might be real, as office buildings, especially in the Southwest, use this system of numbering. A residence is not likely to be listed as a suite number. There may be an "apartment number" listed, and determining the validity of this address will depend on your knowledge of the area. If the address is in the business district, it's unlikely to include an "apartment number. "

♦ Any address that seems to be in use by two or more parties. For example, if you're answering classified ads and two ads with two different names and purposes list the same address, there's a strong possibility that this address is a mail drop. It's virtually certain if part of the address is a suite or box number. For example:

John Smith
292 Swinger Street, #105
Anytown, USA

James Jones
292 Swinger Street, #301
Anytown, USA

It's very unlikely that two people living in the same building would be advertising in the same issue of the same publication.

♦ If you know the locale, watch for incongruities. An address in a business district rings falsely if it's supposed to be the residence of a private party.

♦ A check against listings of mail drops often settles the question conclusively. If the address is local, a quick look in the Yellow Pages, checking under "Mail Receiving Services," will probably disclose it. One important point is that some mail drops tend to be short-lived, appearing and dissolving between issues of the telephone directory.

A new mail drop will not appear and indeed may be extinct by the time the next year's directory comes out. Another way to check this out is by using a computerized telephone directory program. All but the cheapest pro-rams allow you to list all of the telephone numbers by address. This will show you if the address is listed to a real person or a mail service.

♦ For out-of-town addresses, there are two sources to check. One is the computerized telephone directory, which is nationwide. Select Phone and other high-grade CD-ROM directories allow you to check by name, address, or telephone number.

Typing in the name will produce a list of everyone by that name in the area the disc covers. This is why it's wise to limit the search by also including a ZIP code. If the name is very unusual, such as "Z.G. Quackenbush," you don't have to limit the search.

Searching by address will disclose whether there is a mail drop at that address. Keep in mind that in a multi-story building, there will be many individuals or businesses listed.

The final way to search is by telephone number, if one is listed in the advertisement. If the number checks out to an address other than the one listed in the ad, it's probably a mail drop. Remember that the phone number may not check out to the person placing the ad. One reason may be that the person is using an alias for the ad. Another is that the person may be living with someone else, and using that telephone.

A final check is the publication in which the advertisements appeared. There may be a "Services" section, and the address in question may be listed as a mail drop service.

It's important to understand the need for precautions when corresponding. Long-established companies, such as J.C. Whitney, are reputable and are not going to vanish with your money. Ordering anything by mail from a company you don't know has a certain risk.

Another precaution is discretion in disclosing any personal information to anyone whom you don't know. This is especially true of any correspondent operating from a box number. Those who ignore these precautions lay themselves open to embarrassment, blackmail or worse.

Chapter Fifteen:
Tracing You Through The Mail

You may be dismayed at how easy it is to trace you through your mailing address, even if you move. Anyone who moves and who still wants to receive his mail can file a mail forwarding order with the post office. This goes to the post office with jurisdiction over his old address. Postal employees forward any mail sent to the old address to the new one listed. A forwarding order is effective for one year, time enough for anyone to notify his correspondents of his new address.

Before early 1994, it was possible to file a form requesting disclosure of a person's new address and receive a reply through the post office. On January 4, 1994, however, Postmaster General Marvin Runyon stopped this practice because several entertainers and other people had been "stalked," and in some cases harmed, by psychopaths who had obtained their addresses from the post office. Today, disclosure may be only to law enforcement agencies, including the Internal Revenue Service, and may be on an informal basis or with a court order.

However, this new rule doesn't stop anyone who is even slightly sophisticated and has a little common sense. Marvin Runyon's ban on disclosure was merely a "warm fuzzy" to assure the public that something was being done. In reality, it left a large gap, because there are measures to circumvent this ban on new address disclosure to private citizens.

We've seen that law enforcement officers can obtain a court order for the disclosure of your new address if necessary, which is why moving won't solve the problem and keep you beyond scrutiny. Private investigators, without official police powers, use guile instead. Part of the reason guile works is that the post office cooperates with tracers by offering services that fall right in with their needs.

"Certified mail" requires a signature upon receipt. This tells the tracer whether you're still receiving mail. There's another service the tracer can buy. This is the "Show Address Where Delivered" option, in which the postal carrier notes the address where he finally delivered the piece of mail. This is very useful for tracing people who file a change of address form with the post office.

Some tracers, and some law enforcement agencies, use yet another service available from the post office. If there are several people with similar names, and the problem is finding a particular one, the investigator has another trick up his sleeve if he has a sample of the target's handwriting. The tracer can make the postal carrier do his work for him by invoking a requirement that the envelope be delivered only to the addressee, and his signature obtained. This allows a comparison, and greatly simplifies investigative work.

There is an even cheaper way to obtain a new address that requires only a postcard. The sender marks the face of the card "Do not forward. Address Correction requested." You may have seen the "Do not forward. Address Correction requested" legend on junk mail. This saves the junk mailer money by avoiding any forwarding fee, and obtains the new address for his mailing list. This is also useful for private investigators and others who want your new address.

The "Do not forward" instruction is to avoid alerting the target that someone is looking for him. The post office will write the new address on the card and return it to the sender for a nominal fee, which was about 32 cents in early 1996.

Simplifying the investigative task is the key. Most tracers work on a budget, and have limited resources to find their targets. Because their clients are usually creditors and other private parties, they have to charge fairly low fees to make it economical to employ them, and this limits the amount of work they can put in on a "case." This is why they use all sorts of tricks to cut down on the amount of manpower they use.

A money order is another way to trace someone. Receiving a money order requires a signature, and cashing it can also lead to other bits of information, such as the type of I.D. the person cashing it presents. If the recipient deposits it in his bank account, this number will appear on the money order.

Another trick used is the fake personal letter. This is written by someone who claims to be a friend who has not seen the target for a long while, and who wishes to talk over old times. If the target responds, he'll be verifying his identity.

Another variant is the "shotgun" mailing. The U.S. Marshal's Service Fugitive Unit has used this method to trace fugitives economically. There are several ways to do this. One is a mass mailing to the last known address of every fugitive on a list. The mailing is a printed form saying that the person named has just won a car, free trip, or other big-ticket prize in a contest. In some instances, the mailing goes to a relative of the wanted person. The invitation informs the addressee that he has a certain amount of time to return a coupon, or to pick up his prize personally at a certain address. If he returns the coupon, listing his address, he'll soon find unwelcome visitors at his door. If he reports to the address listed, an arrest team will be waiting for him.

There's a simple technique for use in finding someone who has a mail drop. This works only with the type of mail drop where the client comes to pick up his mail, not the mail forwarder. The investigator sends or delivers a large, brightly wrapped package to the mail drop, addressed to the person he's seeking. This technique can work even without a name. It simply requires something like:

Occupant
Box 39
2112 Any Street
Anytown, USA 34567

The surveillant can easily spot anyone who comes out of the mail drop carrying such a parcel. This makes a stakeout from a distance very easy, and allows shadowing the person to his home.[1]

A technique available to law enforcement officers is the "mail cover," as discussed in previous chapters. To trace an individual, the mail cover is placed on his friends ad relatives' incoming mail. This allows investigators to note the return addresses and postmarks on any mail they receive. If the fugitive is foolish enough to send a letter from his true locale, and lists his address on the envelope, he'll give away his new location.

Opening the first-class mail requires a court order, in theory, and this is only granted if there is evidence to obtain by opening the mail. The glimpses of information we've gotten through open sources regarding the behavior of law enforcement officers show that opening first-class mail without a warrant will happen if law officers feel the need for it.

The only hang-up is that any evidence obtained illegally can't be introduced in court. If the investigators are only after a "lead," and not admissible evidence, the field is clear for them.

More important than any evasive maneuvers you take is the person or agency which is looking for you. If you're running away from a creditor or a wife, it's only a civil matter and the most you're likely to have on your trail is a private investigator. Private investigators vary greatly in quality and skill, but the basic fact is that they're private citizens. They have no power to compel a mail drop operator to reveal your address. However, they do use guile, and may be able to trick the mail drop operator into revealing your address .

In some instances, it can become an official matter. If your dispute with your wife involves child support, you can have the law on your trail very quickly. Likewise, a bad debt is a civil matter, but if your creditor can make it look like fraud, the police enter the picture, and they can be very persuasive, even without the formality of a warrant. The threat of having a warrant served on him can persuade a mail drop operator to "roll over" and spill all of the information the police want. If the federal authorities want you, they can be very adept and convincing, and have repeatedly demonstrated their abilities by tracing organized crime members.

Unfortunately, the mail is not the only medium a tracer can use to locate you. Electronic media provide additional avenues of approach, especially if you plug in to one. Even if you have an "unlisted" telephone number, there are ways to discover it.

Telephone Tricks

Private investigators use a variety of telephone scams, known in the trade as "pretext calls," to uncover information.

An investigator will either telephone or visit someone who knows you and who may have your current address, and tell a lie to persuade that person to disclose the information he wants. Many of these lies are oldies, but they still work, which is why investigators keep on using them.

One common pretext is the "unclaimed property" scam. The investigator tells the person that he's working for an attorney who is handling unclaimed property, and that he's trying to find your current location so that he can send you a check for the amount.

A variant on the unclaimed property scam is pretending to be a clerk at the police department property office. The investigator tells the person that the police have recovered a stereo or other valuable appliance that was supposedly stolen from you two years ago, and are trying to locate you so that they may return your property to you.

The "blood donor" scam appeals to the person's altruistic nature. The tracer claims to be an employee of a blood bank, stating that you registered with them and have a very rare blood type. He goes on to say that an accident victim's life is hanging in the balance, and that he urgently needs to locate you so that you can donate a pint of blood. This is a very clever scam, because the urgency doesn't give the target time to think or temporize. Saying "I'll have him get back to you," doesn't solve the alleged "problem."

A very innocent-sounding scam is the "high school reunion" ploy. Claiming to be a former classmate, the investigator telephones your relative or friend and states that he's been unable to locate you to inform you of the impending reunion.[2]

Yet another is the blood-test scam. The investigator pretends to be calling from a doctor's office with the results of the target's HIV test. With the AIDS scare, it's likely that he can convince the person he calls of the seriousness of the situation, and persuade him to disclose what he knows of the target's whereabouts.

Investigators have yet another trick to discover an unlisted number, and this works whether you have a personal unlisted number or if you've taken over another party's number. They rent an 800 number, which you'll recall is one where the called party pays for the call. The telephone company bills the party renting the 800 number, listing each call with the calling number, individually. It doesn't matter if the calling number is listed or unlisted; it appears on the bill.

The investigator's main task is to get you to call that 800 number. He does this with a pretext call to a friend or relative he thinks may be in contact with you. Pretending to be an attorney, he'll tell your friend that he has to get in touch with you regarding a distant relative's estate, or a monetary settlement for an accident you've suffered, and leaves the 800 number with him to relay to you. Once you make that call from your home or office phone, he's got you!

Other Methods

Several companies catering to private investigators have developed huge databases of information that are accessible via computer and modem. These, based only on public records, help the investigator conduct a quick search when time is pressing and more conventional methods, such as the "Address Correction Requested" technique, are too slow.

One vendor of search services advertises that it can provide information based only on a subject's name. This database combines credit header files, publishers' lists, telephone directories, real estate records, demographic information, and street directories. This provides a total of 688 million records, with enough redundancy to zero in on the target. This is available from:

C.D.B. INFOTEK
6 Hutton Center Drive
Santa Ana, CA 92707
Phone: (800) 427-3747

This seems almost too good to be true, and we have to note some limiting conditions. How effective is such a service? One thing they don't tell you up front is that you may receive so many listings that they're useless. Let's look at it from the viewpoint that you are the investigator trying to find a person. If you begin with only your target's name, you may receive an overwhelming flood of information, especially if the name's a common one such as "Smith" or "Jones." Trying to separate the Smith you're seeking from all the other Smiths in the country is an impossible task, if all you have is the name. On the other hand, if the name is something like "Grzybsczbvd," you won't find many entries with that spelling in the database.

This is why, although the company advertises that it can find your target with only his name, it's very helpful to include some "limiters" to narrow the search. A "limiter" is an instruction to list only the Smiths who live on Pearl Street in Denver, for example. Let's see how this works and how you can use it to find a hypothetical fugitive.

You may be seeking someone named "Carter" whom you know left Los Angeles several months ago to go to Idaho, where he has relatives. Idaho has a small population, and this already limits the search. You begin by compiling a list of all the "Carters" in the state, among whom will probably be your target's relatives. If a real estate record shows a recent home purchase by someone with that name, this is probably your target. If it isn't, the rest of the "Carter" list provides some people on whom you can use telephone pretexts to extract the location of your target.

Protecting Yourself: Need To Know

Government security specialists, knowing that foreign powers run very effective espionage services, have learned to minimize the risks by restricting secret information to those who need it to do their jobs. "Need to know" keeps secret information limited and reduces the number of people who might decide to pass information to unauthorized persons. You can make this principle work for you as well. Don't, for example, give out your new whereabouts or address to anyone except the person who will forward your mail.

It's safe to assume that, if you decide to vanish, you'll want to keep in touch only with the most important people in your life, not every casual acquaintance. It won't hurt to let your correspondents know that you're using a mail drop or remailing service so that others cannot trace you. Don't make it appear as if you don't trust them with your new whereabouts. Be honest and up front about it, explaining your reasons for using tight security, and you won't hurt their feelings.[3]

The same goes for telephone numbers. As we've learned from the previous chapter, with modern CD-ROM directories, anyone can discover the address listed with a telephone number. Law enforcement officers can obtain the information directly from the telephone company, even if your number is unlisted, with a court order.

If you absolutely must speak with someone in your old locale or your previous life, be smart, and be discreet. Don't use the old spy-novel trick of giving your friend or relative the number of a pay phone to call so that even if your friend is tricked into disclosing the number, it won't lead to your door. This will frustrate an ordinary citizen and perhaps even a private investigator, but if you're fleeing the law, this trick won't protect you. Police can discover the location of a pay phone, and stake it out at the appropriate time.

Instead, originate all the calls yourself, driving to a city away from your new address and using a pay phone. Call your friends and associates from time to time, to get the latest news, and to ask for any help you need. Tracing telephone calls still takes time, especially if the call is unexpected. Limit your calls to five minutes each, and you'll be perfectly safe. They'll be able to capture your number with Caller ID or other technology, but getting their hands on you will take time. If the discussion takes longer than five minutes, hang up and drive to another location to continue the conversation from another pay phone.

A cellular phone can provide some immunity from tracing, if you adhere to the following procedure:

♦ Pay in cash when setting up your cellular phone service, and use a mail drop address that you're saving for only this purpose. You'll have to pay a hefty deposit if the service provider can't get a positive credit check on you, but the provider won't refuse you service.

♦ Pay monthly bills by money order, to avoid laying the paper trail you would if you used a checking account.

♦ Remember that today it's possible to trace a cellular phone call as well, and a direction-finder can reveal your physical location. Remember the TV coverage of the O.J. Simpson slow-speed car chase? You can avoid being pinpointed if you keep your cellular phone calls short, and avoid having the cellular phone account registered to an address where investigators can find you.

E-Mail

Computer networks and on-line services, such as Internet and Prodigy, provide another way to communicate without being traced. E-mail providers also house e-mail remailing services that strip out the header and other identifying information, then send your message to its destination anonymously. However, some of these anonymous electronic remailers may be operated by government agencies for the express purpose of scrutinizing secret mail. There's a better way.

Sign up with a computer network under an alias, and list a totally false address. Use a bank account under that name for electronic payment of monthly fees, replenishing that account by deposits at an automated teller machine. Once you receive your password, you can obtain access from literally any telephone, even a pay phone, with a laptop computer and modem. Even if you sign your name, nobody can trace you to your physical location because uploading messages takes so little time.

Be Safe!

This is why, if you're evading something serious, it's best not to have any connection between the old and the new. Any trail at all simply lays a path for an investigator to follow. If he has the power of the government behind him, he'll be on your doorstep before you know it.

It's also crucial to side-step the probes investigators may launch your way. Any piece of mail stating you've won a prize and urging you to contact someone is automatically suspect. Any friend or relative who tells you that someone has contacted him and requested that he give you an 800 number to call may be merely a dupe in a pretext scam. Any piece of mail you're not expecting is also suspect, especially if it's registered and requires a signature.

The way to avoid being traced is to be aware of the means investigators can use to locate their targets, and to practice tight security. Understanding tracing techniques helps you to frustrate them. Practicing tight security as a routine lifestyle helps you maintain your cover.

Notes:

1. Anonymous, *New I.D. in America*, Boulder, CO, Paladin Press, 1983 p. 55 .
2. Slade, E. Roy, and Gutz, James R., *The Pretext Book*, Houston, TX, Cloak & Data Press, 1991, p. 34.
3. Budd, Wayne, *The Official Remailing Guide, Eighth Edition*, Eldorado, Ontario, Canada, 1993, p. 6.

Introduction to Part III

Maybe operating a mail drop is your cup of tea. Being self-employed always has its advantages, and the mail drop business has a few more advantages than many others. As a start, you can work very few hours to earn your daily bread. The business tends to run itself. You can also work as many as you wish, if you want to expand the services your business offers. You can even work a mail drop as a sideline or an underground business. This allows you to avoid amputations inflicted by the tax man.

The following chapters will present the nuts and bolts of getting started in mail receiving and forwarding, laying out the merits of different ways of starting up. You'll find that the choice of financing is crucial to the future of your business. You'll also find that day-to-day operations will make the difference between a never-ending hassle and a minor-league gold mine.

Don't let the last phrase fool you, though. You won't become filthy rich with a mail-receiving business. You will, however, have the opportunity to earn a comfortable living with minimal effort.

Chapter Sixteen:
Starting A Mail Drop Buisiness

The big advantage of operating a mail drop is that you need no special skills because managing it is an "entry-level" job. A high school education, as long as you didn't just major in volleyball but actually learned the curriculum, is plenty.

If you're already self-employed, a mail drop can be a sideline. If you own a retail outlet, you might find a few square feet of space to accommodate a stack of lockboxes. This can be profitable, because servicing the boxes takes about an hour a day, depending on the size of the operation.

An attractive aspect of a mail drop service is the cash flow, once the business gets going. Payment of box rental is customarily in advance, which eliminates the risk inherent in many types of businesses.

There are actually two types of mail drops possible. One is the larger, storefront operation, with locked mail boxes and customers who come in to pick up their mail. This requires a large capital investment for equipment, especially if the services include photocopying and other business aids.

The other type is the straight remailing service, in which you simply act as a receiving address for your clients, who never come in to pick up their mail. Instead, you forward their mail to the address they designate.[1] There's practically no overhead on this business, as you can work it out of your home.

Whichever type of operation you choose to start, the important first step is establishing good relations with the local postmaster. An interview with him is desirable, in which you announce your intention and feel him out regarding his attitude. Keep in mind that, although you don't need a license from the post office to open up a mail drop, they can put you out of business by refusing to deliver your mail, which they can do if the postmaster questions your integrity or honesty.

While you're with the postmaster, you can pick his brain for information. He can tell you how many other mail drops are operating in the area, and can also tell you the waiting time for a postal box. You could also find this information on your own. The Yellow Pages will show how many mail drops are listed in the area. Asking a postal clerk at a window will reveal the waiting time for a post office box. There are three ways to start:

Franchises

One franchiser is:

Mail Boxes, Etc.
6600 Cornerstone Court West
San Diego, CA 92121-3795
Phone: (800) 456-0141 (619) 455-8800
Fax: (619) 546-7488

This is the largest mail box franchiser in the world, with over 3,000 operations. Beginning with mail box rentals, franchises also provide other services, such as package receiving and forwarding, photocopy machines, office supplies, printing and stamps, and other business-related services.

The franchiser assists in locating a suitable location, designing the layout to suit the operation, buying or leasing hardware, buying supplies, and negotiating a lease. Mail Boxes, Etc. also provides training in operating procedures, advertising, marketing, and management. Support personnel provide advice, answer questions, and provide assistance.

Mail Boxes, Etc. also offers franchising-cost estimates, providing a bracket between "low" ($94,090) and "high" ($135,927) estimates. Costs include the franchise fee, training, design fee, furniture and equipment, rental, deposits, inventory, prepaid business expenses, and miscellaneous costs.

Another franchiser is:

PAKMAIL Centers of America
3033 South Parker Road Suite 1200
Aurora, CO 80014-2934
Phone: (800) 833-2821, (303) 752-3500
Fax: (303) 755-9721

Pakmail franchises have been somewhat different from ordinary mail drops since Pakmail started in 1983, because the emphasis is on servicing area businesses, providing packing and shipping services as the name implies. They provide package shipping by both parcel post and a variety of private carriers, including overnight-air services. Pakmail centers also provide crating and custom packaging, including large and fragile items, and sell packaging supplies. Mail box rentals are, of course, one of the services, as are fax and photocopies. Mail services include forwarding, receiving, sorting, and metering. Business-support services include binding, laminating, stationery, and business printing.

The franchiser assists in locating a suitable site, remodeling to suit the operation, buying hardware and supplies, and negotiating a lease. Pakmail also provides a week-long training session at its Denver facility. Support personnel help during the opening of the store, providing both on-site training and three days of direct assistance.

Pakmail also offers franchising-cost estimates, providing a bracket between "low" ($55,820) and "high" ($101,633) estimates. Costs include the franchise fee, furniture and equipment, rental, security deposit, inventory, advertising, and miscellaneous costs.

Turn-key

Another way is to buy a "turn-key" business. The producer buys or rents the premises, sets up the furniture and boxes, and provides all the additional equipment and supplies necessary to get you going. He obtains the licenses and takes care of the initial paperwork. Your only task is to sign the forms in the right places. The producer also may provide some basic instruction in how to run the business. You can expect to pay forty-five or fifty thousand dollars. However, the business is then yours. You need only turn the key in the lock and walk in.

A variant on this is buying an established business. This is somewhat uncertain because there has to be an operator willing to sell. There are also good and bad points about buying an ongoing business. One good point is that the equipment will be somewhat depreciated. A bad point is that you'll be paying a premium, because most business owners charge for "good will," the trade that they've built up during their ownership.

One source for "turn-key" mail drops is:

Mail & More
4747 East Elliot Road, Suite #29
Phoenix, AZ 85044
Telephone: (602) 893-3278

Start Your Own

This means buying the equipment, renting the premises, and getting the entire operation underway without help. If you already have experience in mail drop operations, you don't have to pay a franchiser for training. You may not benefit from the volume discounts that franchisers advertise, but you get to keep everything you would otherwise have to pay the franchiser. On the other hand, you have to make all of the decisions yourself. As we'll see, help is available, but without paying huge franchising fees. Equipment manufacturers are happy to provide advice to potential customers, and other organizations sell operating manuals for small fees.

In rare instances, it's possible to find a good deal on second-hand equipment. Usually, because mail drops are an expanding field, it's necessary to buy new from one of several suppliers. Like franchise operators, equipment suppliers in this field offer practical help to get started. This is both common and logical because teaching the business is simple. There's just not that much to learn. Suppliers also realize that teaching someone who plans to start up is creating a new customer for their products.

Some sources for lock-boxes and further information on starting up on your own are:

Postal Center
8033 Sunset Blvd.
Los Angeles, CA 90046
Telephone: (213) 650-0009

Salsbury Industries
1010 East 62nd Street
Los Angeles, CA 90001
Telephone: (800) 323-3003
(213) 232-6181
Fax: (213) 232-7021

Salsbury Industries manufactures mailboxes in clusters of 30 for the smallest size, and 8 for the largest. Doors are die-cast brass, each door with a clear glass window, and two keys for each 5-pin cylinder lock. Combination locks are optional on the two smaller door sizes.

Security Manufacturing Corp.
815 South Main
Grapevine, TX 76051
Telephone: (800) 762-6937
(817) 329-1600
Fax: (817) 481 -3993

Security Manufacturing provides postal boxes in a variety of sizes, with solid doors indented at the bottom for application of identifying labels. Box modules come with five-pin cylindrical locks. Also available are a passport/ID photo camera, a simulated video camera to enhance security, and a key machine for those interested in making their own keys or operating a key-making service as a sideline.

One organization that offers an operating manual for a mail drop that also offers other services is:

Associated Mail and Parcel Centers
705 School Street
Napa, CA 94559
Telephone: (800) 365-2672
Attn: Charmaine Fennie, Executive Director

Membership costs $160 per year. The association is a resource center and lobbying group for independent mail drop operators, and offers training materials, a toll-free "helpline," and seminars covering the operation of mail drops. The Association has arranged member discounts from equipment suppliers, provides freight discounts, overnight-air discounts, credit card and long distance discounts, shipping insurance, and business owners insurance. A monthly newsletter reports on industry developments, and provides a forum for sharing new ideas. The Association also sells books related to operating mail drops. Some are:

The Diversified Business Services Center. The 1993 edition of this book provides a huge amount of nuts-and-bolts information for anyone who wants to start up a comprehensive private mail service. A few of the highlights are:

- Toll-free numbers for several commercial package services.
- Checklists for opening and closing the business.
- A guide to hiring employees.
- A draft of an employee policy manual.
- Floor plans.
- Mini-manuals on operating sidelines, such as photocopying.

This book is obtainable through the Association for $40.

Promoting Your Mail/Parcel Business, price $25. This volume discusses the most effective ways of advertising.

The Complete Parcel Shipper, price $30. This manual explains techniques of wrapping and shipping parcels, and includes UPS and post office rate charts.

Security Manufacturing, listed above, provides an operating manual, *Turning Mail Boxes Into Cash Boxes*, covering how to get into the business, how much money is necessary to begin operations, office layouts, installing boxes, daytime operation, training office help, and an assortment of forms needed to operate a mail drop.

Location

This is a critical point, and one with many ramifications. The first point to consider is the general area. Ideally, it should be one with a great demand for mail drops. This suggests a population of at least 10,000 people within three to five miles. One favorable feature is a post office with a waiting list for boxes. Experience has shown that a mixed residential and business district offers the best prospects. Another favorable factor is high-rent affluent apartments in the area. Of course, if many private operators already exist, there will be little business left for you.

The exact site of your mail drop is crucial. There should be easy access and lots of parking. A small strip center with very limited parking will strangle your business. A better location is on a two-way street with a good amount of traffic, preferably a street people travel on their way to and from work or shopping. A "good" address is an advantage, which means don't locate it in a waterfront or ghetto district. It's also better to be at street level than upstairs, for easy access by hurried customers. A storefront is ideal.

If you set up at the end of a strip center, you'll be able to offer customers drive-through window service. This can be very important for busy clients.

There are contradictory opinions regarding whether your mail drop should be close to or far from the post office. Some people believe that the best location is a few doors from the post office, if space is available, but it's also possible to make a case for a more remote location. This is because you stand to gain from customers who don't want to make the drive to the post office, and if the post office is far from a population center, you should go where potential customers are. Also keep in mind that one of your major selling points is customer convenience, and a location in a heavily congested downtown area is not convenient.

All things considered, it's not truly important whether you're close to or far from a post office. You're not really in competition with the post office, because the types and variety of services you offer far outclass the limited services a post office provides. If you intend to operate only a forwarding service, location isn't important.

An essential point is adequate staffing. You should have enough people on hand so that customers don't have to wait in line the way they do at the post office. One important reason for patronizing your mail drop is to avoid waiting at the post office, where insolent clerks take their time and seem to almost enjoy keeping postal customers waiting in long lines. Someone who has just come from the post office, where clerks shut their windows as more customers were getting in line, is a good prospect for your business if it's obvious that you provide immediate service.

Depending on the size of your operation and the extra services you plan to provide, you'll need between 500-1,000 square feet of floor space. When you include a copy machine, displays for stationery and other office supplies, and mailboxes, even 1,000 square feet may not be enough.

An important point is to discover the attitude of the local postmaster. The local postmaster should not be hostile to private mail drops, in theory, because a mail drop is also a postal customer. However, this may change because in 1995 U.S. Postmaster General Marvin T. Runyon made a plea for "any kind of legislation that will let us run more like a business." These aren't empty words. Behind this plea is a program to expand post office services into areas formerly operated only by private enterprise. In this, the U.S. Postal Service has an unfair advantage, because U.S. legislation makes the delivery of first-class mail a U.S. Postal Service monopoly, and now the post office is seeking to infringe on services provided by private businesses.

Already, the post office provides packaging services, prepaid telephone cards, information kiosks, and other cutting-edge services and products. The new "postal stores" are an attempt to compete with office supply outlets and private mail centers. Operating at an unfair advantage because it doesn't have to pay income or corporate taxes, doesn't collect sales taxes, and is truly above local laws, the post office poses an economic threat to mail drop operators.

Arranging a meeting with the postmaster will tell you what his attitude is. Although he has to abide by the postal regulations, his attitude can be positive and helpful. It can also be obstructive, and if this is so, it's better to choose another location.

Similarly, meet with the local businessmen. If they have a mind-set against mail drops and see no need for them, it's a negative factor. A lot depends on local circumstances. In some instances, businessmen don't use mail drops to conduct business, but as individuals they may use them heavily for sexually oriented and other private mail.

Other good indicators are a high rate of theft from the area's mailboxes. Apartment-house mailboxes may be targets for thieves. The flimsy unlocked boxes in front of many one-family dwellings are ripe for pilferage.

A crucial point regarding location is always to use a street address. Never operate out of a post office box as some mail drop operators do. This is a dead giveaway that there's something being hidden, and some clients will go elsewhere to avoid this revealing feature.

An important construction detail is a concrete floor, because lock-boxes are heavy and a wood floor over a basement might be too weak. However, modern commercial construction is usually done in anticipation of housing a business with lots of floor stress, such as a hardware or grocery store.

The lease can be crucial. One important positive feature of a mail drop is stability, because customers don't want to be notifying their correspondents of address changes every few months. Customers value stability, so go for a long lease. Anything under a year isn't worth a second look, and a three- to five-year lease is better.

Layout

The basic plan for a lock-box operation is to have a lobby and a "back shop" for your work and storage area. The lobby should be neat and uncluttered, because if you plan to offer 24-hour access, anything you include for decoration will be subject to theft or vandalism. A self-service copy machine might be worthwhile if there's little risk of theft and if the traffic justifies it. A work counter for the convenience of customers is important. A Dutch door arrangement giving access to the back can serve as a counter during the day.

Because lobby access exposes you to theft, you have to consider security. Some mail drops use closed-circuit TV cameras connected to a VCR to tape anyone who enters. Putting the cameras in a conspicuous, but inaccessible, location will deter some vandals and thieves.

Naming the Business

The name you choose will be limited by the type of business it is and the need to avoid any of the names owned by the U.S. Postal Service. You can't call it a "Post Office," nor can you call the boxes "Post Office Boxes" or "P.O. Boxes.[2]

The best bet is to call your business "Mail-something." You may find that others in your area have thought of this too, as a quick look in the Yellow Pages will show. Whether or not business names are legally registered in your state, it's better to avoid using one already in use by someone else, in order to avoid confusion. The exception is if you're operating a franchise, such as "Mail Boxes, Etc." You'll be required to name your business as the franchiser designates.

Brainstorm a bit to find another name. Run over in your mind the possibilities coming from describing the usefulness of your mail drop. Try names such as these on for size:

CONFIDENTIAL MAIL
YOUR PRIVATE MAIL
MAIL CONVENIENCE CENTER
NO-WAIT MAIL CENTER
YOUR MAIL RECEIVER
YOUR MAIL OFFICE
YOUR MAIL DEPOT
COMPREHENSIVE MAIL SERVICES
SECRET ADDRESS
YOUR PRIVATE ADDRESS

If your intention is to aim your service towards businessmen, selling them on convenience and service, you might choose a name that reflects this:

BUSINESSMAN'S CENTER
THE BUSINESS SERVICE CENTER
COMPREHENSIVE BUSINESS CENTER

Letterheads and Business Cards

You'll need some cards and letterheads for normal business correspondence and as handouts. You'll also need some brochures describing your services. Envelopes are essential, and you'll need these in at least two sizes. One is the normal #10 business size, for correspondence with clients and potential clients. The other is a larger size, perhaps 6″ x 9″ or 9″ x 12″, for forwarding clients' mail.

Discretion is important, and some of your clients will appreciate this. It's important that you have only the street address and not the business name on any of the envelopes. This is to avoid tipping off anyone who sees the envelope that the client is getting anything from a mail forwarder or mail drop. Discretion is necessary not only when forwarding mail. If you have a client in a remote area, whom you bill for services periodically, it's indiscreet to send him his bill in an envelope that obviously comes from a mail forwarder. In especially sensitive cases, you may wish to discuss this with the client. He may prefer that you send any correspondence to him in a plain envelope.

Attracting Customers

One quick way to find customers is to poach the post office's clients. Although government regulations forbid placing advertising posters on government property or soliciting on the premises, direct mail advertising is both legal and efficient. You simply mail an advertising leaflet to everyone who has a post office box nearby. Addressing is simple. You just go to your local post office and note where the box numbers begin and end. Then you address each piece of mail as:

Occupant
P.O. Box #12345
Anytown, USA, 67890

The appeal should be on the basis of convenience and the extra services you provide that the post office doesn't. Some post offices have coin-operated copy machines in the lobby. Big deal! So do supermarkets. As a mail receiver, you can offer your customers more comprehensive services, as outlined in the chapter on seeking out a mail drop.

Here's a sample "selling" letter that you can copy and use if you take the approach described next:

ACME MAILING COMPANY
123 ANY STREET
ANYTOWN, USA 12345
Telephone (123) 456-7890

Dear Mr. Businessman:

This is to introduce the Acme Mailing Company, a new service that offers area businesses convenience in communications. Post office boxes are almost unavailable locally, and the next nearest post office is a half-hour drive. We can have a box for you within minutes. You will also have a prestige address, not just a "P.O. BOX" number.

We can save you money, because you can phone in to check if any mail has arrived for you, which saves you useless trips. We also offer you savings in one-stop business services. At Acme, we can meet your photocopying, United Parcel Service, Federal Express, and Western Union needs all at once. Acme also offers messenger service, money orders, dictation and transcription.

Enclosed is our rate card. If there's something you need that you don't see, just ask. Come in and see us anytime.

Sincerely,

Another approach is to solicit the businessmen in the area by mail or in person. Emphasize the convenience, and if they are not using a post office box, mention the early availability of mail you provide, instead of their waiting for the mail carrier to arrive later in the day. Point out the comprehensive services you provide.

If you decide to solicit private individuals, convenience is again the key. Some of these will come in as walk-in customers. Explain that call-ins to find out if they have any mail are free, and that this offsets the rate differential by what they save in time and gasoline.

Advertising with classified ads is another choice. This is mostly worthwhile for soliciting out-of-town clients. There are people who want addresses in other parts of the country, and to reach these you need to insert classified ads in national publications.

Generally, the sleazy weekly tabloids, adventurer's magazines, and mechanical magazines have the best pulling power. Don't overlook the sexually-oriented mags, because they're naturals for this. There's no point in listing them here, because some might not be available in your area and advertising rates are subject to change. The best way to find out the publications' addresses and rates is to pick some up at a newsstand. To save money, find the ones you can at your local library and copy the necessary information out of them. As the library probably doesn't carry the sleazier publications, it'll be necessary to buy them where they're available.

It's not enough to pick up a publication and copy the address. Take a good look at the classified section to see how many other mail drops advertise in that publication. You can be sure that the ones with many mail drop ads are the ones with "pulling power" for this sort of business.

There are some publications to avoid. Biker magazines and those catering to the drug culture can be undesirable because you don't need the complications that this class of customers will bring you. The "narcs" who enforce the drug laws have very uncharitable attitudes and may see you only as a willing accomplice if your boxes are used for mailing drugs.

Financing

This is a point on which we see a lot of bad or useless advice. The basic needs in starting a business of any sort are enough money to set up the operation and to keep it and the owner going until it breaks even. Think of "starting capital" and "operating capital." "Starting capital" buys the equipment and sets you up. "Operating capital" pays the bills until the business starts to pay for itself.

Depending on the area of the country in which you live, the local rentals, and the size of the business, starting a storefront operation will cost roughly twenty thousand dollars. If you want only a simple mail-forwarding business, you can work from a rented room or office, or even your home, and start with much less. An agency limited to mail forwarding doesn't need lockboxes, which are the biggest items of capital equipment.

If you've got enough money to set yourself up and to live for a few months, you're in an excellent position. If not, you can either borrow or scale down your expectations. Buy less initial equipment and rent more modest premises.

Tied in with this are obtaining a business loan and franchising the operation. A franchise sometimes requires less investment. Obtaining a small business loan can be very difficult, because banks and other lenders prefer to lend money for expansion to a going concern rather than to bankroll a beginner. This is where private investors are the worst. Despite the legend that businessmen take daring risks in search of large returns, this is only public-relations puffery. Those involved in "venture capital" are very timid. The truth is that they prefer to take no risks at all.

The central issue is that the more of the business you own yourself, the higher proportion of the income you get to keep. If you own it all, you'll start breaking even sooner than if a certain fee has to go to the franchiser and another percentage to the bank.

The Final Decision

The shape of your business will be mainly what makes you feel comfortable. It's best to keep the operation at a level you can handle without strain, because one of the prime reasons for going into business for yourself is to be free from the emotional attrition and general hassle that often go with being a wage worker. If you like a quiet life, you'll probably feel more comfortable with a minimal business, offering private mail receiving and few allied services. This will allow you to keep your shop open fewer hours per week than otherwise possible.

If, on the other hand, you like the hustle and bustle of a busy shop, enjoy meeting and dealing with people, and want to earn as much as possible, the other choice is for you. Offering many tie-in products and services will, on the average, earn you more money from customer contacts. You'll have to be open more hours to service your customers, or hire someone to work an overlapping shift, but it will be worth it.

Notes:

1. Michael R. Ives, *The Mail Drop Manual*, Huntington Beach, CA, Benchmark Press, 1982, p. ii.
2. *Ibid.*, pp. 20-21.

Chapter Seventeen: Operating A Mail Drop Business

Once the business is started, there's a need for policies and procedures to keep it running.

Pick Up or Wait for Delivery?

Some clients want their mail early. For these, you may have to pick up your mail at the post office loading dock. There is no charge for this service, but this may not be necessary if mail deliveries to you are early enough in the morning to help you keep your clients happy. In any case, you can't get the mail until the carrier assigned to your route has finished sorting it.

Another way is to rent a box at the local post office, which will cost you the price of the box rental. As a rule, the post office puts the mail up in its boxes long before deliveries begin to street addresses. The big disadvantage of picking up is that you have a fictitious box number. There's no box physically there, as all mail for your operation goes into a postal sack which you pick up, but the box number is the address your clients must use.

For those who prefer discretion, your street address is the better choice. These patrons will have to tolerate their mail arriving when the mail carrier gets there. The advantage to you is that the mail carrier does all of the work: delivering your incoming mail, and picking up outgoing mail.

An important caution is to be very careful about returning mail that is not for you or any of your clients, especially if the local post office staff is in any way hostile to you. It's illegal to misdirect or divert mail, and discarding an envelope addressed to someone else, even if unknown to you, can lead to a prosecution. When you get such mail, and you surely will, stamp it "UNKNOWN AT THIS ADDRESS" and return it.

Rental Policy

Always collect rents in advance. To avoid overly transient clients, rent only in three-month minimum periods. This makes each rental worthwhile, and allows a slight extra profit if you specify in the rental agreement that there is no refund for unused rental on cancellation. If anyone cancels before his period is up, you're free to rent the box to someone else.

You'll need printed "Rent Due" forms to slip into customers' boxes about ten days before the current rentals expire. A firm policy on rentals is one which you can and should enforce strictly. Ten days' notice of rent due is about right. Another ten days' grace period is also reasonable. This should be clearly spelled out on the rental contract. You can make use of the "Rent Due" forms for reminding the customer by hand-lettering "OVER" on top of the word "Due." This saves an extra printing charge.

If the client has not paid the next period's rent within this time, you should return his mail to the post office marked "NO LONGER AT THIS ADDRESS-RETURN TO SENDER."[1] It's illegal to hold his mail hostage for payment. In any event, returning it to the custody of the post office accomplishes the same purpose: he doesn't receive it.

It's unwise to charge a lock-box customer for accepting a parcel for him if the volume is low. Consider this as part of the service and your competitive edge over the post office. By the same token, you should never lay out your own money to accept C.O.D. parcels for a customer. He may not want the shipment, which leaves you stuck.

Offering Discounts

Discounts for long rentals are worthwhile. Offering six months' rent for the cost of five is one way. Another way to use a discount is as a "bird-dog" fee. Offering customers a free month's rent for each referral may encourage them to pass the word, and you don't have to pay until you collect.

Certified and Registered Mail

There are special concerns regarding certified and registered mail. You ought to be aware of them for several reasons. One reason is that postal regulations dictate special handling and storage for registered and certified mail, including a vault for overnight keeping. Another is that I.D. is required from the recipient, and this may put off some of your clients. Yet another is that certified mail, especially that which has a "show address where delivered," is a technique used by investigators to trace people. Therefore, to avoid complications, the simplest policy is to refuse such mail. For the sake of good customer relations, this must be spelled out in the rental agreement. If some certified or registered mail arrives, accept only the yellow notice from the mail carrier and place it in the customer's box.

Keys

There are two ways to provide 24-hour lobby access for clients. One is to have a combination lock on the front door, changing it at intervals to deny access to former customers. Another is using a keyed lock. Combination locks require remembering the combination, while keyed front-door locks are easier to use. A partition divides the lobby from the rest of the premises.

Unless you have combination locks on the boxes as well, your customers will need keys. This is generally the best way to go, because most people have more trouble with combination locks than they do with key locks. There should be a modest deposit on the key, enough to allow you a profit, because this is actually a service for the client. Some customers don't turn in their keys when they stop paying for the service, which means that you have to make a new key. In any case, you should change the lock on the box at the end of a rental, for security's sake. This is because the client may have duplicated his key. You can use the same lock on another box later.

There may also be a reason to issue a lobby key, if you have partitioned off the rear work area. This allows clients 24-hour access to their boxes, and is desirable from the viewpoint of clients who work odd hours or who want to pick up their mail discreetly and infrequently.

Issuing keys is so much a part of the business that it pays to have your own key machine and a stock of blanks. With this capital equipment, it's good business to put it to use earning more money. With the machine already on hand, a stock of commonly-available blanks is all that's necessary, and with a charge of two dollars per key this provides a slight extra income.

Other Services

One way to accommodate customers and build good will is to sell stamps. Customers will appreciate being able to buy stamps in your shop without standing in the long lines that post offices all seem to have. A prominent sign advertising that you sell stamps will bring more people into your storefront operation, including potential clients. Don't expect to make a profit on these. It would create a bad taste to tack a premium onto the price of the stamps, although some mail drop operators do so on the basis that they're also selling convenience.

The opportunity for tie-in sales exists. Envelopes, packages of writing paper, pads and pens are worthwhile items to stock. You can sell these at a good profit, unlike stamps, and provide the customer with materials he'd otherwise have to get at a stationery-supply outlet.

Other services mail drops offer are laminating, résumé writing and printing, gift wrapping, rubber stamps, greeting cards, fax services, passport photos, and notarizing documents. A photocopy machine allows customers to make their own copies, and provides multiple copies of résumés you may prepare for a client.

Some customers need a telephone message service. This isn't an "answering" service that picks up on their office or home lines. This is a separate number which you offer at a price lower than the answering services in your area. It requires a line which you reserve for only these incoming calls. You simply answer this line with the last four digits of the number, because there will be several clients. The response is always the same:

"Mr. Jones is not in right now. May I take your name and number and have him return the call?"

You'll need a telephone answering machine if you want to provide 24-hour service. Round-the-clock coverage is important to some customers.

Serving as a sub-station for United Parcel Service, Federal Express, and other carriers can bring in extra income. The purpose is to make the most of the time that the customer's in your store, and to foster a dependency on the services you offer. Federal Express and Western Union can be very profitable, especially because they furnish the equipment.

Handling Western Union money orders is also an extra-charge service. This service can be popular in college towns, where students request money from home.

Handling outgoing packages for clients can be very profitable. You can tack on a premium for handling, especially if you offer to package it for your customer. During the holiday season, there's an opportunity to catch some of the spillover from the regular carriers, where lines are long with the heavy traffic.

Mail forwarding can also be profitable. This depends a lot upon customers' needs. Some may want their mail forwarded to them daily, while others are satisfied with weekly shipments. For individuals, you may feel that the forwarding is included in the box rental if you run a store-type operation. Postage is extra, of course. .

When dealing with a business, it's wise to be careful because some unexpected developments may take place. A company may send you several thousand advertisements to mail out. If they're pre-addressed and stamped, there's no problem. You simply deliver them to the post office with your other outgoing mail. Replies to the ads may be voluminous, however, and unless the client comes in to pick up the replies, forwarding them to the company will be costly.[2] This is why any client who wishes his mail forwarded should have an account on deposit with you to pay for postage involved. The amount will vary with the volume. A private individual should have at least ten dollars deposited at the outset. A company should have one hundred dollars. The exact amount depends on the situation and certainly is negotiable, but it should be written policy that forwarding of mail stops when the account runs out.

Other opportunities for profit can be found in acting as an agent for other types of businesses. If you have a good relationship with the owner of a print shop (Who does your brochures?) you may be able to get a discount, and you'll make your money by brokering jobs from the customer to the printer. An arrangement with a photo processing lab can bring you a few extra dollars by using your store as a deposit and pick-up station for photofinishing. Because many customers need another roll of film when they drop one off for processing, stocking a small supply can bring in more money from tie-in sales.

Hours

By far, the best and most profitable operation is the one offering 24-hour access to the boxes. This requires dividing the premises into two parts: the lobby and the "back shop." At the outset, you might find yourself spending long hours, from sunrise to sunset, manning the store to sign up new customers. You might even be open Saturdays and Sundays. Once your boxes are fully rented, there's no need for such long hours anymore. As long as clients can use their lobby keys (for which you charge a modest fee) to gain access to their boxes when they wish, you don't need to be there more than about six or eight hours a day, and certainly not on weekends.

Problems and Frauds

Anyone operating a mail drop should be aware that some sharp con artists prey on mail drops and mail forwarders. One scam is the "lost merchandise" trick. Here's how it works:

The con artist hires a mail drop that offers forwarding and also has a street address. He orders expensive equipment and merchandise, such as electronic equipment or rare books, and orders the mail forwarder to send it on to him via parcel post. This is not normally insured unless the client requests it. The con artist then refuses payment, claiming that he never got it. Because the mail drop operator signed for it from the carrier, he's stuck for the cost.[3]

The way to avoid being victimized this way is to follow a hard policy of never forwarding any merchandise without insuring it. The customer, of course, pays the cost.

Another fraud is to use the mail drop for ordering merchandise and not paying for it. This can happen if the renter uses fake I.D. and is therefore hard to trace. The tip-off is if most of the mail coming to a particular box is from book and record clubs, or from mail-order vendors.

Another scam is to use a mail drop as a return address for filing false income tax returns with the Internal Revenue Service. For the sake of speeding refunds, the IRS issues checks before fully checking out the returns, and if you see a number of checks from the IRS coming to one of your clients, there's reason to suspect that this is his game.

Yet another is defrauding credit card companies. You can expect some of your clients to use the mail drop to establish false I.D., but an occasional one may use false I.D. as a means to set up spurious credit accounts and rip off banks and credit companies. An unusual number of bills from credit card companies can indicate this. This is especially true if you see any with "SECOND NOTICE" or a similar legend stamped on the envelope.

It's important for the mail drop operator to be aware of the possible frauds that dishonest clients can work, using him as an unwitting accomplice. Because the operator is usually unaware of his clients' business dealings, police and postal inspectors are fairly tolerant and don't consider him an accomplice. However, a lot depends upon how many such incidents there are. An operator who makes it too easy for his mail drop to be used for frauds may find the post office refusing to deliver his mail.

One way to help avoid problems, or to at least, cover yourself if any occur, is to have a paragraph in the rental contract that reads something like this:

"Customers should be aware that this contract is valid only for legal use of the mails. Both the customer and the operator are obliged to abide by postal regulations. The client guarantees not to use this mail receiving service for any fraudulent or illegal purpose."

With careful planning, and following the precautions other mail drop operators have found valid, you should be able to avoid most of the possible problems that can plague the operator.

Notes:

1. Worldwide Remail Association, *The Remail Business*, Richmond, IN, 1983
2. Hunter, T.H.E., *Mail Service Centers*, Winston-Salem, NC, Hunter-Hall & Associates, 1984, pp. 6-7.
3. "C.W.L.," *Mail Drops*, Pasadena, CA, The Technology Group, 1985, pp. 4-5 .

Chapter Eighteen:
An Underground Mail Drop

In some cases, it's both possible and profitable to run an underground mail drop. There are two advantages to this:

1. You operate out of sight of the post office and other authorities, and can accommodate customers without filling out the Form 1583. This total secrecy enables you to charge a premium price.
2. You get to keep more of what you earn because you pay no income taxes. You also don't apply for any business license from your local government, and you don't pay any filing or incorporation fees.

Starting and running your underground operation are quite different procedures than those involved in operating an aboveboard one. Not everyone can do this. The first and most important requirement is a "cover" occupation, because the postal carriers will notice an unusual amount of mail made out to different names coming to your address. If the carrier is simply not curious, you might be able to get away with this for a long time. However, there's no assurance that the carrier won't quit, get transferred, or go on vacation. His replacement might be a gung-ho curious type who reports anything unusual to the postal inspectors. It's not illegal to run a remailing service without the post office's knowledge, but they'll start bugging you for signed copies of Form 1583, and might even pass your name along to the Internal Revenue Service for special attention.

If you run a rooming or boarding house, you have a good cover for accepting mail for different people. The mail carrier will be used to delivering envelopes addressed to a variety of names, and won't even think about the number and the turnover because normally the population of a rooming house is constantly changing.

Another opportunity exists if you're the superintendent or manager of an office building. Personal mail often comes for tenants and their employees, and sometimes doesn't list the company name. It's not hard to get to know the mail carrier, and persuade him or her to deliver such problem envelopes to you, who will offer to run down the addressees. More likely, the carrier will look you up when there's an unknown addressee.

You'll probably find your clientele according to your location. A businessman would not want the return address of a rooming house, unless he's acting as an individual. If, on the other hand, he's into illicit sex, the address would be fine. Another consideration is the location of correspondents. If they're local they would probably know that the area and the address should not be incongruous. If a client's running a mail-order business or the like, with clients all over the country, location won't be important.

"Advertising" has to be entirely by word of mouth. There's no need for business cards or letterheads, and any mail you forward will be in totally plain envelopes. Along with saving the cost of printing, it's best not to show that any sort of commerce is going on, and printed envelopes are a tip-off, no matter how discreet the printing .

Your business is likely to start with someone else's initiative, such as an acquaintance asking you to receive mail for him. One of your tenants might ask you to receive mail for him under an alias. It's easy to accommodate him and earn money with the right tactics. A good answer to such a request is:

"Yes, sir, be glad to do that. I already do that for a couple of others in the building and charge them only fifteen a month for the service."

Payment should always be cash, and always in advance. It's futile and foolish to set up credit accounts. As a purely practical matter, you're likely to run into a lot of deadbeats among those who seek truly underground secret addresses, and it's best to use the leverage you have to enforce payment. Holding their mail hostage may seem like a stern measure, but so is cheating someone who provides an important service.

Another important point is that you may attract a larger proportion of people engaged in illegal activities. While it may not bother you to think that your service is being used by someone evading taxes or an angry wife, you may have different feelings about someone working drugs through your mail drop.

A Small Business

It's worthwhile to keep your underground remailing business small for the sake of a low profile and for your convenience. The low profile is important for any underground operator. It's also vital to your clients' interests. Keep in mind the investigative storm that will come down on you and on every one of your clients if you're found out.

If the dollar volume is low, this will be extra protection if ever the Internal Revenue Service gets "on your case." IRS agents are interested in production, retrieving big bucks from large evaders, not the nickel-and-dime business that eats up their time and produces little reward. They won't waste precious hours pushing an intensive investigation or prosecution for the few tax dollars they can collect from you. The only exception to this is if they decide to make an "example" of you. Their term for picking someone out for special treatment is "selective enforcement."

Another reason is that you cannot allow the underground business to take too much time away from your main responsibility. This is why it must remain a part-time affair.

Chapter Nineteen: Ethics

Unfortunately, mail drops have acquired sleazy reputations because of the activities of a few clients. You may hesitate to become involved because of this negative image.

How responsible are you for the activities of your clients? This question may nag at you, partly because of the image problem, but also because you may worry about being indicted as a co-conspirator if any of your clients' actions end up in prosecutions.

Let's look at the law first. It's a federal offense to open first-class mail or to interfere with delivery in any way. You don't know what a client's mail contains, and if you suspect that he's doing anything illegal, you can't take any active steps. If you try to find out by opening his mail, you're in trouble, not he.

The second point is that clients hire your service for its discretion. You have to show a professional lack of curiosity about their business. This is a good attitude to maintain, because otherwise you can be wasting time chasing your suspicions endlessly.

What if the indications of illegal activity become unmistakable, so blatant that you feel that you can't put up with them any longer? You may realize, as pointed out in the preceding chapter, that one of your clients is into something definitely fraudulent.

You have two alternatives. One is to handle it informally, and hold a private conference with your client to discuss the legality of his actions. If his answers aren't satisfactory, you might ask him to take his business elsewhere. This is workable, although some people might become very angry at the veiled accusations.

The other way is to notify the local postal inspector. This takes it out of your hands and places the responsibility squarely on him.

We see, then, that your responsibility is limited. You can't play policeman, although you can't totally ignore problems areas, either. As a practical point, if there are too many scams run out of your mail drop, it will start to appear that you're a participant. This is why you have to walk the middle ground.

APPENDIX I:
MAIL DROPS IN THE 50 LARGEST U. S. CITIES

Albuquerque, New Mexico:

Albuquerque Mail Center
1925 Juan Tabo NE, Suite B
Albuquerque, NM 87112-3359
(505) 296-8111

Mail Boxes, Etc.
10131 Coors Blvd. NW
Albuquerque NM 87114-5334
(505) 897-4358

Atlanta, Georgia:

Mail Box Rentals
595 Piedmont Avenue
Atlanta, GA 30308-2433
(404) 872-2026

Mail Boxes, Etc.
4279 Roswell Road NE
Atlanta, GA 30342-3700
(404) 256-3948

Austin, Texas:

Mail & Parcel Services
4032 South Lamar Blvd.
Austin, TX 78704-7971
(512) 442-1188

Mail Center USA
2021 Guadalupe Street
Austin, TX 78705
(512) 478-4747

Baltimore, Maryland:

Mail Boxes, Etc
822 Guiford Avenue
Baltimore, MD 21200
(410) 783-1555

Mail-Rite
3500 Parkdale Avenue
Baltimore, MD 21211-1442
(410) 383-0007

Boston, Massachusetts:

Mail Boxes, Etc.
304 Newbury Street
Boston, MA 02115-2832
(617) 437-9303

Mail Boxes, Etc.
360 Huntington Avenue
Boston, MA 02115-5096
(617) 373-2090

Buffalo, New York:

Mail Boxes, Etc.
23 Lafayette Square
Buffalo, NY 14203-1800
(716) 852-3166

The Mail Room
559 South Park Avenue
Buffalo, NY 14204-2627
(716) 856-3622

Charlotte, North Carolina:

Mail Boxes, Etc.
1235 East Blvd.
Charlotte, NC 28203-5870
(704) 342-1950

The Mail Center
1400 East Morehead Street
Charlotte, NC 28204-2926
(704) 358-3585

Chicago, Illinois:

Mail and More
6427 West Irving Park Road
Chicago, IL 60634-2437
(312) 282-6060

Mail Boxes, Etc.
7144 North Harlem Avenue
Chicago, IL 60631-1097
(312) 792-9595

Cincinnati, Ohio:

Mail Boxes, Etc.
5465 North Bend Road
Cincinnati, OH 45211
(513) 662-9211

Mail Boxes, Etc.
1232 West Kemper Road
Cincinnati, OH 45240-1618
(513) 742-9490

Columbus, Ohio:

Mail Boxes & Services
1601 West 5th Avenue
Columbus, OH 43212-2303
(614) 488-1863

Mail Boxes, Etc.
3000 East Main Street
Columbus, OH 43209-3712
(614) 237-5770

Dallas, Texas:

Mail Box Express
8365 Park Lane
Dallas, TX 75231-6607
(214) 696-1222

Mail Boxes, Etc.
1920 Abrams Road
Dallas, TX 75214-3915
(214) 827-5200

Denver, Colorado:

Mail Boxes, Etc.
1685 Colorado Blvd.
Denver, CO 80220-1067
(303) 753-0888

Mail Room
85 South Union Blvd.
Denver, CO 80228-2207
(303) 986-3941

Detroit, Michigan:

The Mail Depot
2950 Holbrook Street
Detroit, MI 48212-3512
(313) 871-2240

Mail Plus
17366 Harper Avenue
Detroit, MI 48200
(313) 885-1766

El Paso, Texas:

Mail & More
601 North Cotton Street
El Paso, TX 79902-5732
(915) 533-6245

Mail Boxes, Etc.
9155 Dyer Street
El Paso, TX 79924-6424
(915) 751-3334

Fort Worth, Texas:

Mail Call, Inc.
3001 Halloran Street
Fort Worth, TX 76107-5085
(817) 737-7151

Mail It and More
7455 South Hulen Street
Fort Worth, TX 76133-7358
(817) 263-5524

Fresno, California:

Mail & More
5730 North 1st
Fresno, CA 93650
(209) 447-8341

Mail Boxes, Etc.
385 West Shaw Avenue
Fresno, CA 93704-2647
(209) 225-6153

Honolulu, Hawaii:

Mail Boxes, Etc.
1960 Kapiolani Blvd. Ste 113
Honolulu, HI 96826-3975
(808) 955-7361

The Mail Exchange
1164 Bishop Street, Ste. 124
Honolulu, HI 96813-2800
(808) 524-1164

Houston, Texas:

Mail Box
9327 Katy Freeway, #B
Houston, TX 77024-1512
(713) 464-1233

Mail Boxes, Etc.
2476 Bolsover Street
Houston, TX 77005-2546
(713) 529-4132

Indianapolis, Indiana:

Mail Boxes, Etc.
133 West Market Street
Indianapolis, IN 46204
(317) 236-0009

The Mail Room
5230 West 16th Street
Indianapolis, IN 46224-6431
(317) 244-0117

Jacksonville, Florida:

Mail and More
1836 West 3rd Street
Jacksonville, FL 32209-7257
(904) 247-8614

Mail Boxes, Etc.
2771-25 Monument Road
Jacksonville, FL 32203
(904) 646-4941

Kansas City, Missouri:

Mail & More
2631-A NE Vivion Road
Kansas City, MO 64100
(816) 454-2424

Mail Boxes, Etc.
4741 Central Street
Kansas City, MO 64112
(816) 561-7411

Long Beach, California:

Mail N More
2150 East South Street
Long Beach, CA 90805-4457
(310) 790-1800

The Mail Room
5520 East 2nd Street
Long Beach, CA 90803-3943
(310) 438- 1152

Los Angeles, California:

The Mail Bag
1283 La Brea Avenue
Los Angeles, CA 90019-1627
(213) 938-0101

Mail Box Rentals Plus
11659 Santa Monica Blvd.
Los Angeles, CA 90025-2931
(310) 575-3588

Memphis, Tennessee:

Mail Boxes, Etc.
714 Germantown Pkwy.
Memphis, TN 38101
(901) 757-1144

Mail Boxes, Etc.
6025 Stage Road
Memphis, TN 38134-8374
(901) 385-8701

Miami, Florida:

Mail Box Rentals, Inc.
7907 NW 53rd Street
Miami, FL 33166-4603
(305) 592-4955

Mail N More
7426 SW 117th Avenue
Miami, FL 33183-3816
(305) 596-6448

Milwaukee, Wisconsin:

Mail Boxes, Etc.
544 East Ogden Avenue
Milwaukee, WI 53200
(414) 273-7780

Mail Mart
6506 West Capitol Drive
Milwaukee, WI 53216-1665
(414) 463-6245

Minneapolis, Minnesota:

Mail Boxes, Etc.
5021 Vernon Avenue South
Minneapolis, MN 55436
(612) 920-1024

The Mailbox Company
7725 North Riverdale Avenue
Minneapolis, MN 55430
(612) 560-0712

Nashville, Tennessee:

The Mail Box
330 Franklin Street
Nashville, TN 37201-2219
(615) 370-0300

The Mail Room
1024 17th Avenue South
Nashville, TN 37212-2202
(615) 329-9520

New Orleans, Louisiana:

Mail Boxes
4324 Chef Menteur Highway
New Orleans, LA 70126-4920
(504) 944-1499

Mail Boxes, Etc.
6003 Bullard Avenue
New Orleans, LA 70128-2834
(504) 245-7885

New York, New York:

Mail Alternatives Plus
461 W. 49th Street
New York, NY 10019-7203
(212) 399-0575

Mail Box City Ltd .
510 Brighton Beach Avenue
Brooklyn, NY 11235-6404
(718) 891-7654

Oakland, California:

Mail Boxes & More
408 13th
Oakland, CA 94601
(510) 763-1165

Mail Boxes, Etc.
360 Grand Avenue
Oakland, CA 94610-4840
(510) 835-1209

Oklahoma City, Oklahoma:

Mail & Business Center
107 South Sooner Road
Oklahoma City, OK 73110
(405) 672-4850

Mail & Stuff
4922 NW 23rd Street
Oklahoma City, OK 73127-2369
(405) 947-7513

Omaha, Nebraska:

Mail America, Inc.
1360 Ellison Avenue
Omaha, NE 68110-1140
(402) 493-8400

The Mail Room
5062 South 108th Street
Omaha, NE 68137-2314
(402) 331-2014

Philadelphia, Pennsylvania:

The Mailroom
8001 Castor Avenue
Philadelphia, PA 19152-2701
(215) 745-1100

Postal Plus
7107 Frankford Avenue
Philadelphia, PA 19092
(215) 335-0444

Phoenix, Arizona:

Mail & More
4747 Elliot Road
Phoenix, AZ 85044-1627
(602) 893-3278

Mail Boxes, Etc.
9201 North 29th Avenue
Phoenix, AZ 85051-3468
(602) 944-6336

Pittsburgh, Pennsylvania:

Mail Boxes, Etc.
7 Market Square
Pittsburgh, PA 15123
(412) 391-1911

Mail Boxes, Etc.
414 South Craig Street
Pittsburgh, PA 15213-3709
(412) 687-6100

Portland, Oregon:

Mail Boxes, Etc.
16869 SW 65th Avenue
Portland, OR 97281
(503) 598-7662

Mail Call
8407 NE Fremont Street
Portland, OR 97220-5150
(503) 252-3967

Sacramento, California:

The Mail Bag
3018 J Street
Sacramento, CA 95816-4402
(916) 443-5812

The Mail Centre
3313 Julliard Drive
Sacramento, CA 95826-3510
(916) 383-0888

St. Louis, Missouri:

Mail Boxes, Etc.
7536 Forsyth Blvd.
St. Louis, MO 63105-3436
(314) 862-3700

Mail Parcels & More
12788 Olive Blvd.
St. Louis, MO 63141-6211
(314) 878-3020

San Antonio, Texas

Mail Boxes, Etc.
10004 Wurzbach Road
San Antonio, TX 78230-2214
(210) 697-8481

Mail & Parcel Center
16608 San Pedro Avenue
San Antonio, TX 78232
(210) 496-1335

San Diego, California:

Mail Boxes, Etc.
9450 Mira Mesa Blvd.
San Diego, CA 92126-4850
(619) 689-9151

Mail Call Plus
4019 Goldfinch Street
San Diego, CA 92103-1820
(619) 296-2971

San Francisco, California:

Mail Boxes 4 You
1230 Market Street
San Francisco, CA 94102-4801
(415) 621-1991

Mail Boxes, Etc.
564 Mission
San Francisco, CA 94107
(415) 495-6963

San Jose, California:

Mail Boxes, Etc.
4960 Almaden Expressway
San Jose, CA 95118-2000
(408) 264-8800

Mail Center AM
6172 Bollinger Road
San Jose, CA 95129-3000
(408) 253-8192

Seattle, Washington:

Mail & Parcels Plus
2802 East Madison Street
Seattle, WA 98112-4800
(206) 860-8711

The Mail Box
3213 Wheeler Street
Seattle, WA 98199-3200
(206) 285-4843

Toledo, Ohio:

Mail Vault, Inc.
1455 South Reynolds Road
Toledo, OH 43615-7400
(419) 389-1212

Mail Vault North
39 West Alexis Road
Toledo, OH 43612-3682
(419) 476-6500

Tucson, Arizona:

Mail & More
1171 East Rancho Vistoso Blvd.
Tucson, AZ 85737-9107
(520) 825-8848

Mail Boxes, Etc.
4072 East 22nd Street
Tucson, AZ 85711-5334
(520) 747-9800

Tulsa, Oklahoma:

The Mail Box
8177 South Harvard Avenue
Tulsa, OK 74137-1600
(918) 481-3281

Mail Boxes, Etc.
5103 South Sheridan Road
Tulsa, OK 74145-7627
(918) 627-8388

Virginia Beach, Virginia:

Mail and More
309 Aragona Blvd.
Virginia Beach, VA 23462-2700
(804) 490-2211

Mail Depot
105 North Plaza Trail
Virginia Beach, VA 23452
(804) 463-4107

Washington, DC:

Mail Boxes, Etc.
611 Pennsylvania Avenue SE
Washington, DC 20002
(202) 543-0850

Mail Boxes, Etc.
4401 Connecticut Avenue NW
Washington, DC 20016
(202) 244-7299

Appendix II:
Select List Of Private Vaults
By State

Arizona:
Keep It Safe, Inc.
7925 Oracle Road
Tucson, AZ 85704-6316
(520) 742-0091

Mountain Vault
11820 N. Cave Creek Road
Phoenix, AZ 85020-1326
(602) 943-9796

Arkansas:
Citizens Investment Services, Inc.
200 S. Elm Street
Hope, AR 71801-4391
(501) 777-2313

California:
Datasafe
South San Francisco, CA 94080
(415) 875-3800

Datavault United States Deposit Co.
Newport Beach, CA 92660
(714) 760-1145

First Alarm
545 Brunken Ave BB
Salinas, CA 93901
(408) 424-1111

FirstAlarm
1111 Estate Drive
Seacliff, CA 95003
(408) 476-1111

California (continued):

International Depository
498 Valencia Street
San Francisco, CA 94103-3415
(415) 863-4417

Security Vault & Storage, Inc.
394 Tasconi Ct.
Santa Rosa, CA 95401-4653
(707) 571-7777

Sloan Vaults Inc.
5455 Kearny Villa Road
San Diego, CA 92123-1105
(619) 576-9400

Connecticut:

The Vault
1212 East Putnam Avenue
Riverside, CT 06878-1431

Florida:

Datavault
1801 S. Federal Hwy.
Delray Beach, FL 33483-3321
(407) 272-7233

Fort Knox Public Vault, Inc.
1406 NE Capital Circle
Tallahassee, FL 32301
(904)878-1100

Permavault
100 South Biscayne Blvd.
Miami, FL 33010
(305) 373-4431

Intervault, Inc.
3562 N. Ocean Blvd.
Fort Lauderdale, FL 33308-6752
(305) 565-7233

Georgia:

C. B. &T.
406 West Main Street
Manchester, GA 31816-1657
(706) 846-8471

Illinois:

71st Street & Jeffrey
   Safe Deposit Co.
7054 S. Jeffrey Blvd.
Chicago, IL 60649-2016
(312) 288-1000

A Michigan Safe Deposit Co.
30555 Northwestern Hwy.
Farmington Hills, Ml 48334-3160
(810) 626-6944

Illinois (continued):
Lemont Currency Exchange, Inc.
1116 State Street
Lemont, IL 60439-4235
(708) 257-8900

Iowa:
MIC Data Services
124 S. Fiorst Street
Oskaloosa, IA 52577-3126
(515) 673-8303

Kansas:
Campbells Marine Inc.
Lincoln, KS 67455
(913) 436-2338

Louisiana:
Safe Place
3490 Drusilla Lane
Baton Rouge, LA 70809-1866
(504) 927-0131

Massachusetts:
Boston Safe Deposit & Trust Co.
1 Boston Place
Boston, MA 02108-4403
(617) 722-7697

Michigan:
Depository, Inc.
30900 Telegraph Road
Birmingham, MI 48009
(810) 540-1255

Nevada:

Southwest Executive Vaults
2929 S. Maryland Parkway
Las Vegas, NV 89109-2217
(702) 792-2220

Vault, Inc.
5050 Meadowood Mall Circle
Reno, NV 89502-6543
(702) 689-7911

New Hampshire:

Personal Storage Units
116 Lyme Road
Hanover, NH 03755-6600
(603) 643-8282

New Jersey:

New Jersey State Safe Deposit Association
1921 Delaware Avenue
Whiting, NJ 08759
(908) 350-5577

New York:

China Safe Deposit Co
225 Park Row
New York City, NY 10038-1165
(212) 964-5296

LSB Associates, Inc.
55 East Avenue
Lockport, NY 14094-3785
(716) 434-6621

Univault
115 East 57th Street
New York City, NY 10022-2049
(212) 644-0124

Zurich Depository Corp.
1165 Northern Blvd.
Manhasset, NY 11030-3048
(516) 365-4756

North Carolina:

American Safety Deposit, Inc.
135 W. Morehead Street
Charlotte, NC 28202-1815
(704) 377-9615

First Safe Deposit Corp.
3506 University Drive
Durham, NC 27707-2636
(919) 493-8502

Oklahoma:
Vault Management, Inc.
6929 South Lewis Avenue
Tulsa, OK 74136-3914
(918) 496-1048

Pennsylvania:
First National Safe Deposit Corp.
York Road West
Jenkintown, PA 19046
(215) 576-1300

Tennessee:
Custom Security, Inc.
4794 Summer Avenue
Memphis, TN 38122-4732
(901) 685-1500

Nashville Vault Company, Ltd.
226 3rd Avenue North
Nashville, TN 37201-1623
(615) 244- 1140

Texas
Causey's Coin & Jewelry
1806 Layton Street
Fort Worth, TX 76117-5437
(817) 831-0074

Fortress For Safekeeping
3417 73rd Street
Lubbock, TX 79423-1125
(806) 793-3472

Laredo Vault, Inc.
410 E. Hillside Road
Laredo, TX 78041-3291
(210) 722-3420

Stout Safe Storage, Inc.
2300 7th Street West
Amarillo, TX 79106
(806) 374-8698

Strongbox
2002 11th Street
Beaumont, TX 77703-4910
(409) 892-7233

Utah:
Crossroads Plaza Shopping
50 S. Main Street
Salt Lake City, UT 84144-0103
(801) 535-1000

Highland Storage
4010 Highland Drive
Holladay, UT 84124-1617
(801) 278-4785

Virginia:

Arlington Security Vault
2499 N. Harrison Street
Arlington, VA 22207-1611
(703) 237-1133

United Security Vaults
4719 West Broad Street
Richmond, VA 23230-3207
(804) 355-9175

Washington

American Coin and Vault
5523 N. Wall Street
Spokane, WA 99205-6433
(509) 326-7512

Econo-Vault of Factoria
13120 SE 30th Blvd.
Bellevue, WA 98004
(206) 746-4800

Feland Safe Deposit Company
201 A Street NW
Auburn, WA 98001-4928
(206) 939-7880

West Virginia:

Financial Consultants, Inc.
US Rt. 60 & 2nd Street NW
Kenova, WV 25530
(304) 453-4141

Summit Holding Corp.
129 Main Street
Beckley, WV 25801-4615
(304) 256-7262

Wisconsin:

Fortress For Valuables
12021 W. Bluemound Road
Wauwatosa, WI 53226
(414) 258-2858

Appendix III: Secretarial Services In The 50 Largest U.S. Cities

Note: Strangely, not all large cities have secretarial services. Where none are listed, the nearest are provided.

Albuquerque, New Mexico:

Home Office
2730 San Pedro Drive NE
Albuquerque, NM 87110-3365
(505) 884-3497

Juan Tabo Garden Offices
3900 Juan Tabo Blvd NE
Albuquerque, NM 87111-3984
(505) 298-1010

Atlanta, Georgia:

CE Secretarial Services
175 West Wieuca Road NE
Atlanta, GA 30342-3254
(404) 303-1007

Crowne Office Suites Downtown
100 Peachtree Street N.W.
Atlanta, GA 30303
(404) 880-3370

Austin, Texas

Confidentially Yours
7701 North Lamar Blvd.
Austin, TX 78752-1000
(512) 451-5089

Echelon Executive Suites
9430 Research Blvd.
Austin, TX 78759
(512) 345-2994

Baltimore, Maryland:

Office Works
4423 Harcourt Road
Baltimore, MD 21214-3321
(410) 254-9120

Secretary Supreme
3008 Spalding Avenue
Baltimore, MD 21215-5121
(410) 664-7623

Boston, Massachusetts:

Bac-up Business Services
99 Chauncy Street
Boston, MA 02111-1703
(617) 482-9848

Office Plus
60 State Street
Boston, MA 02109-1803
(617) 723-5900

Buffalo, New York:

Alphabyte Business Services
1140 Delaware Avenue
Buffalo, NY 14209-1682
(716) 884-2023

Paragon Secretarial Services
Statler Building
Buffalo, NY 14200
(716) 847-1260

Charlotte, North Carolina:

Ace Secretarial Service
2017 East 7th Street
Charlotte, NC 28204-3335
(704) 333-5073

Executive Center Services
5000 Executive Center Drive
Charlotte, NC 28212-8826
(704) 535-5040

Chicago, Illinois:

HQ Business Centers
70 West Madison Street
Chicago, IL 60602-4205
(312) 214-3100

Your Secretarial Service
715 East 104th Place
Chicago, IL 60628-3001
(312) 468- 1046

Cincinnati, Ohio:

Community Secretarial Service
4100 Executive Park Drive
Cincinnati, OH 45241-4026
(513) 563-2525

Concise Clerical Service
2005 Dallas Avenue
Cincinnati, OH 45239-4752
(513) 931-8832

Columbus, Ohio:
Bexley Office Services
458 North Cassady Road
Columbus, OH 43205
(614) 253-0022

Complete Secretary
4601 North High Street
Columbus, OH 43214-2043
(614) 262-8000

Dallas, Texas:
AMS Secretarial Service
5910 North Central Expressway
Dallas, TX 75206-5125
(214) 891-6363

Cambridge Secretarial
3939 Belt Line Road
Dallas, TX 75244-2217
(214) 247-0553

Denver, Colorado:
A & A Business Services
2394 South Broadway
Denver, CO 80210-5007
(303) 871-8370

Specialized Office Services
1903 South Downing Street
Denver, CO 80210-4124
(303) 777-1371

Detroit, Michigan:
A-1 Business Communications
18557 East Warren Avenue
Detroit, Ml 48200
(313) 885-4040

ESI
615 Griswold Street
Detroit, Ml 48226-3901
(313) 965-2424

El Paso, Texas:
Gal Friday
9434 Viscount Blvd.
El Paso, TX 79925-7053
(915) 593-2333

Pams Business Services
3901 North Mesa Street
El Paso, TX 79902-1541
(915) 545-2252

Fort Worth, Texas:
Always An Answer
4802 Highway 377 South
Fort Worth, TX 76116-8897
(817) 244-2852

Multi-Star Services
3016 May Street
Fort Worth, TX 76110-6513
(817) 924-0500

Fresno, California:

Alpha Omega Services
1255 West Shaw Avenue
Fresno, CA 93711-3716
(209) 222-7474

Bullhead Ink
8187 North Del Mar Avenue
Fresno, CA 93711-6016
(209) 449-7609

Honolulu, Hawaii:

Headquarters Companies
2200 Main Street, Ste 500
Wailuku, HI 96793
(808) 242-2828

Home Secretary
73-1204 Ahulani Street
Kailua Kona, HI 96740-9420
(808) 325-5579

Houston, Texas:

Best Secretarial Services
1155 Dairy
Houston, TX 77079
(713) 493-2378

Devon Office Park
17300 El Camino Real
Houston, TX 77058-2743
(713) 486-4300

Indianapolis, Indiana:

Abs-Accent Business Service
8011 Castleton Road
Indianapolis, IN 46250-2004
(317) 842-6633

Executive Office Services
24 H, 8910 Purdue Road
Indianapolis, IN 46268-1170
(317) 872-8289

Jacksonville, Florida:

EBC Office Center
4190 Belfort Road
Jacksonville, FL 32216-1459
(904) 296-7221

Offices Plus
4191 San Juan Avenue
Jacksonville, FL 32210-3398
(904) 388-8938

Kansas City, Missouri:

AAA Secretarial Service
3312 Broadway Street
Kansas City, MO 64111-2402
(816) 531-4615

Burke Secretarial Services
721 NE 76th
Kansas City, MO 64100
(816) 468-6850

Long Beach, California:

Business Office Support Service
5530 East 2nd Street
Long Beach, CA 90803-3924
(310) 439-4151

Omega Business Service
3520 North Long Beach Blvd.
Long Beach, CA 90807-3905
(310) 595-1022

Los Angeles, California:

Barbara's Secretarial Service
1680 Vine Street
Los Angeles, CA 90028-8855
(213) 463-2476

CW Executive Services
8939 Sepulveda Blvd.
Los Angeles, CA 90045-3605
(310) 568-1024

Memphis, Tennessee:

Bartlett Professional Secretary
2840 Bartlett Road
Memphis, TN 38134-4519
(901) 377-0424

EBC Office Centers
5865 Ridgeway Center Parkway
Memphis, TN 38120-4006
(901) 682-4934

Miami, Florida:

Aventura Executive Offices
20801 Biscayne Blvd.
Miami, FL 33180-1430
(305) 931-1616

Braddock Business Services
334 Minorca Avenue
Miami, FL 33134-4304
(305) 448-3295

Milwaukee, Wisconsin:

DJS Typing Service
6200 North Bay Ridge Avenue
Milwaukee, WI 53217-4327
(414) 962-8119

GM Secretarial Services
4810 South 76th Street
Milwaukee, WI 53220-4360
(414) 282-2829

Minneapolis, Minnesota:

Central Services
1415 North Lilac Drive
Minneapolis, MN 55427
(612) 544-5102

Edina Executive Services
5200 Willson Road
Minneapolis, MN 55424-1332
(612) 922-0920

Nashville, Tennessee:

Executive Plaza Suites
3200 West End Avenue
Nashville, TN 37203-1330
(615) 783-1600

Office Services
5008 Granny White Pike
Nashville, TN 37220-1404
(615) 371-1633

New Orleans, Louisiana:

A-1 Secretarial Services
1100 Poydras Street
New Orleans, LA 70163-1100
(504) 569-2059

A-1 Secretarial Services
639 Loyola Avenue
New Orleans, LA 70113-3125
(504) 592-2615

New York City, New York:

The Mechanical Secretary
10816 72nd Avenue
Flushing, NY 11375-5350
(718) 268-3292

Roman & Roman Typing Service
346 East 205th Street
Bronx, NY 10467-4410
(718) 519-0321

Oakland, California:

Evelyns
1814 Fruitvale Avenue
Oakland, CA 94601-2411
(510) 534-5472

HQ Business Centers
1300 Clay Street
Oakland, CA 94612-1425
(510) 464-8000

Oklahoma City, Oklahoma:

Added Assets
1312 Sovereign Row
Oklahoma City, OK 73108-1800
(405) 947-6221

Professional Suite
100 Park Avenue
Oklahoma City, OK 73102-0806
(405) 236-1544

Omaha, Nebraska

American Office Services
302 South 16th Street
Omaha, NE 68102-2209
(402) 341-0919

Execu-Suites
12020 Shamrock Plaza
Omaha, NE 68154-3537
(402) 333-4610

Philadelphia, Pennsylvania:

CDR Associates
100 Arch Street
Philadelphia, PA 19106-2203
(215) 413-3810

Elite Secretarial Services
2200 Friendship Street
Philadelphia, PA 19419-1323
(215) 338-2112

Phoenix, Arizona:

Arizona Secretarial
4501 North 12th Street
Phoenix, AZ 85014-4202
(602) 266-3160

Lecota Executive Suites
706 East Bell Road
Phoenix, AZ 85022-6640
(602) 992-0699

Pittsburgh, Pittsburgh:

Affler Secretarial Services
2987 Babcock Blvd.
Pittsburgh, PA 15237-3234
(412) 931-5464

The Executive Touch
9 Parkway Center
Pittsburgh, PA 15123
(412) 928-9703

Portland, Oregon:

Executive Secretarial Services
5835 NE 27th Drive
Portland, OR 97211-6136
(503) 287-8676

Shared Secretarial Services
4380 S.W. Macadam Avenue
Portland, OR 97201-6403
(503) 274-6264

Sacramento, California:

Biz Serve, Inc.
9211 Beatty Drive
Sacramento, CA 95826-9702
(916) 368-0206

Capitol Secretarial Services
4th & J
Sacramento, CA 95814
(916) 444-0349

St. Louis, Missouri:

A Plus Business Service
10205 Gravois Road
Saint Louis, MO 63123-4029
(314) 843-8959

Executive Suite Services
1515 North Warson Road
Saint Louis, MO 63132-1111
(314) 423- 1737

San Antonio, Texas:

Ande & Associates
84 NE Loop 410
San Antonio, TX 78216-5820
(210) 366-2556

The Office
8811 Rain Valley Street
San Antonio, TX 78255-2165
(210) 698-3314

San Diego, California:

Executive Assistant
6136 Mission Gorge Road
San Diego, CA 92120-3413
(619) 284-1040

Kathie's Typing Service
5402 Ruffin Road
San Diego, CA 92123-1318
(619) 576-1277

San Francisco, California:

Burges Sterrett
2107 Van Ness Avenue
San Francisco, CA 94109-2536
(415) 441-4433

Kricks Office Services
1438 Valencia Street
San Francisco, CA 94110-3708
(415) 826-3284

San Jose, California:

Debbie's Secretarial Services
675 North 1st Street
San Jose, CA 95113
(408) 294-1833

ESQ Business Service
31 North 2nd Street
San Jose, CA 95113
(408) 280-2020

Seattle, Washington:

A Word Express
1218 3rd Street, Suite 510
Seattle, WA 98104
(206) 292-9696

Beasley Secretarial
228 N E 174th Street
Seattle, WA 98155-4934
(206) 367-9200

Toledo, Ohio:

Action Secretarial Service
608 Madison Avenue
Toledo, OH 43604-1108
(419) 246-5762

Divers Secretarial Services, Inc.
5650 West Central Avenue
Toledo, OH 43615-1519
(419) 536-7181

Tucson, Arizona:

ASAP Secretarial Services
7601 North Andover Drive
Tucson, AZ 85704-7101
(520) 575-8410

M&M Typing Services
100 North Stone Avenue
Tucson, AZ 85701-1511
(520) 624-0365

Tulsa, Oklahoma:

Ann's Typing
5558 South 79th East Place
Tulsa, OK 74145-7846
(918) 665-7593

International Business Center
7136 South Yale Avenue
Tulsa, OK 74136-6373
(918) 494-9041

Virginia, Beach, Virginia:

ADIA Personnel Services
192 Ballard Court
Virginia Beach, VA 23462-6538
(804) 499-0688

Birdneck Executive Centre
1206 Laskin Road
Virginia Beach, VA 23451-5263
(804) 428-2192

Washington, DC:

Arbor Office Suites
1919 Pennsylvania Avenue N.W.
Washington, DC 20006
(202) 736-2100

Office Specialists
1025 Connecticut Avenue N.W.
Washington, DC 20037
(202) 466-7100